First Aid for Underwater Finds

Wendy Robinson

Archetype
Publications

Nautical
Archaeology
Society

in association with the
NATIONAL MARITIME MUSEUM

The decorations on the section dividers are reproduced by permission of the National Maritime Museum.

I. Sea monsters: top – from Olaus Magnus, *Historiae de Gentibus Septentrionalibus, c.* 1550 (NMM neg. A2709): bottom – from Waghenaer's *Mariner's Mirror*, 1584 (NMM neg. A6865)
II. Fish and whale, after Waghenaer (NMM negs D2306-1, D2306-7)
III. Compass rose from a 'Study of Navigation' of *c.* 1726 (NMM Ms, NVT 21: neg A5605)
IV. Compass rose/calendar from Ribeiro's *Portugaliae Monumenta Cartographica*, 1529 (NMM neg. A8384)

Published jointly by Archetype Publications Ltd and the Nautical Archaeology Society

Archetype Publications Ltd
6, Fitzroy Square
London W1P 6DX
Tel. 44(171) 380 0800
Fax 44(171) 380 0500

Nautical Archaeology Society
c/o 19 College Road
HM Naval Base
Portsmouth PO1 3LJ
Tel. 44(1705) 818419

First published 1998

ISBN 1 873132 66 2

Typeset by Kate Williams, Swansea.
Printed and bound by Ashford Colour Press Ltd. Gosport, Hants.

Contents

Foreword

by Richard Ormond, Director, National Maritime Musem

In 1981 the National Maritime Museum published Wendy Robinson's *First Aid for Marine Finds* – a 40-page pamphlet of basic advice on a topic then becoming increasingly important with the growth of both recreational diving and underwater archaeology. Nearly twenty years on, the importance of the underwater heritage and the risks to which it is subject worldwide, especially with advances in deep-sea technology, are now even more widely recognised. While the National Maritime Museum is itself no longer directly involved in maritime archaeological work, it continues to support the aims of those who are, both in the protection of historic shipwrecks, and in preserving and interpreting the material evidence of the past that they represent, for the general public benefit. Sound conservation practice is a vital part of this process, and we are delighted to welcome this much enlarged 'second edition' of Wendy Robinson's work. The degree to which it has expanded since 1981 is both a measure of the development of the field in that time and of her own as a leading authority in it.

Preface

This book has been written as an update of *First Aid for Marine Finds* (Robinson 1981). It is a response to the need for immediate and practical advice on the preservation of finds and while condemning unnecessary disturbance and indiscriminate removal, it directs the reader on how to deal with legitimately recovered material until the advice of a qualified conservator can be sought.

Intended to supplement texts on the theory, practice and techniques of archaeology underwater, this update has been broadened to include fresh and stagnant water sites – river, lake, pond, well, etc. – where the chemistry, biology, salinity and other physical characteristics may be diverse, but that have in common with seawater the waterlogged environment and potential for anaerobic sediments that make the preservation of submerged finds possible.

The range of advice is also extended to material that cannot be strictly classified as 'artefact' or 'object' and that may easily be overlooked or destroyed, such as foodstuffs, environmental remains, waste products and other incidental debris. These are an essential part of the archaeological and ecological record and make their own unique contribution to our historical and cultural heritage.

First-aid techniques described in the book are designed to be passive in nature, the aim being preservation with the least interference with the state of the find. This can generally be achieved by physical controls, the use of chemicals or biocides being reserved for the rare occasions when no alternatives exist. Health, safety and environmental issues are also addressed, with every attempt to suggest substances or products that can be used and disposed of with minimum risk to the user or the environment. In addition, clean, natural water, from sea, lake or river is advocated, wherever possible, as an alternative to tap or purified water.

The book is written for non-specialist practitioners who have a sincere and genuine interest in preserving finds so that they can be recorded, studied and published and thereby added to the archaeological and cultural record. No initial conservation expertise has been assumed, but it is hoped that genuine practitioners will be encouraged to extend their knowledge and skills by seeking further advice, attending training courses such as those run in many parts of the world by the Nautical Archaeology Society (NAS) or by working under the guidance of a qualified conservator. Specialist conservators will recognise treatments that have been published in more detailed and critical contexts (such as *Studies in Conservation*, *The International Journal of Nautical Archaeology*, and many conservation monographs), and will hopefully appreciate the greater emphasis on initial guidance given here. For more detailed accounts of laboratory procedures readers are referred to *Conservation of Marine Archaeological Objects* (Pearson 1987) and *The Elements of Archaeological Conservation* (Cronyn 1990). Full details of underwater archaeological methods and techniques, including recording, drawing and photography can be found in *Archaeology Underwater: The NAS Guide to Principles and Practice* (revised edition) published by NAS (1995).

Methods described in the book are set in a global context. In this respect I have started with my own experience of underwater sites in Britain, Sicily and Mombasa, but drawn much more on the detailed accounts of conservation procedures published and related by archaeologists and conservators throughout the world. I am most grateful to those authors. I also gratefully acknowledge the encouragement of Alan Aberg who, as Chairman of NAS, initiated the project and gave his continued support. My thanks are also extended to Anne Allen and Valerie Fenwick for reading and correcting early revisions, Ian Oxley for supplying ideas, Veronica Robbins, HM Coastguard and Receiver of Wreck, for her advice and contribution to the section on legislation, James Black at Archetype Publications for putting it all into order and the National Maritime Museum for giving its support. I also had valuable discussions and correspondence with John Carpenter, Helen Cox, Martin Dean, Peter Gesner, Christine Ianna, Robert Janaway, Mark Jones, Annabel Lawrence, Mark Lawrence, Louise Mumford, Ernest Perry, and Justin Ruhge. For the photographs, I am grateful to Boyd Harris, the National Museum of Antiquities of Scotland, the National Museum of Wales, the Mary Rose Trust, Colin Martin, Mark Redknap and Philip Robertson. Finally, I would like to thank my parents, Mary and Leslie, and daughters, Holly and Laura, for their help and support, always.

Wendy Robinson
Skipton

I

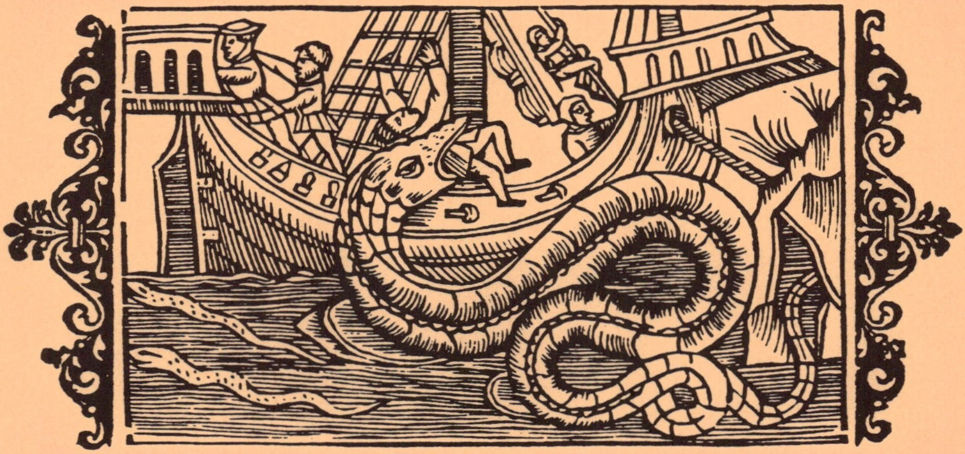

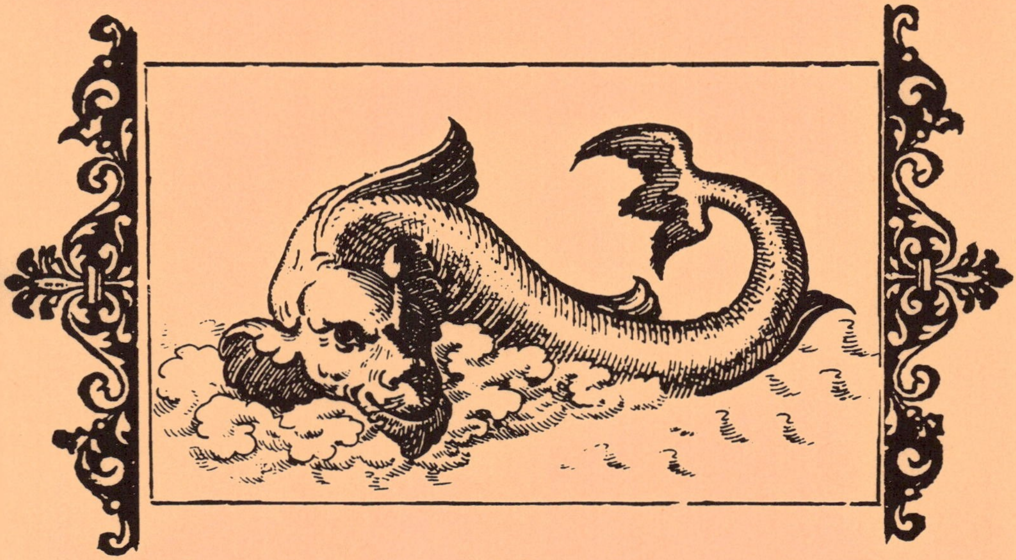

1 Introduction

Anyone who discovers an underwater site has a very special responsibility. By making the discovery you have formed a direct link with our past, and all prospects of enhancing our knowledge and understanding of life and past events lie in your hands. Such sites are part of our cultural heritage and you have become one of the guardians of our past, so it essential that you take the right course of action. All too often finds from underwater sites are indiscriminately removed and, in the process, important archaeological contexts are destroyed. Another mistake is over-zealous cleaning, which may remove important evidence about the find's history or usage and destroy the protective coatings that enabled it to survive in the first place. Some finds are discarded when they are found to have little or no monetary value and, after the novelty of discovery has worn off, others are neglected and allowed to fall into decay. All this is to be condemned as nothing short of vandalism.

Finds are irreplaceable cultural resources, part of our national and international heritage, and each has a significant part to play in the

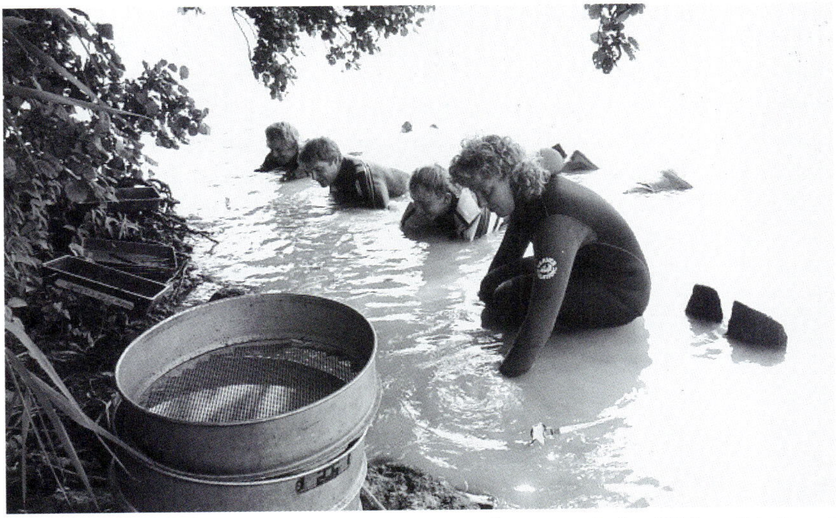

Excavations at the medieval crannog site, Llangorse Lake, Wales. (National Museum of Wales)

intricate jigsaw puzzle of the past. Finds can survive for thousands of years under water and will continue to do so unless they are disturbed. The mere act of discovery does not justify their removal. Too often it heralds destruction, so it is the duty of any finder to prevent this and ensure that the right course of action is taken. If not, the legacy of a bygone age will be destroyed for ever.

On occasion, and working under the supervision of a qualified archaeologist, there may be no alternative but to record and raise the find. Archaeological methods and detailed recording techniques are covered in other books (see, for example Dean *et al.* 1995). Here we are concerned with the stabilisation of finds and their need for treatment in the critical period between location and the start of proactive conservation, when first aid is essential.

What is first-aid conservation?

First-aid conservation has many definitions but here it is taken to be the attempt to stop finds deteriorating between the time of their initial discovery and the point when more active treatments can begin, which may be anything from a few days to years or even decades later. First-aid conservation starts the moment the find is located.

First aid can include 'pre-conservation', preventive action, stabilisation and preservation. The overriding consideration is to achieve stability with minimum intervention on the part of the practitioner, and least change in the state of the find. While active conservation should only be undertaken by those trained in the profession, first-aid treatments can be carried out by those first taking responsibility for the find, even before its exact ownership is known.

First-aid processes include correct lifting, recovery, packaging, transportation, storage, recording and documenting finds until they can be placed in the safe hands of a qualified conservator. There may be occasions, for example when urgent archaeological information is needed on site, when techniques such as preliminary cleaning, desalination (removal of salts), drying and even mending may be required. These procedures are risky and must only be done under supervision to avoid jeopardising the success of future conservation treatments or destroying any associated archaeological evidence. Even then, it is essential to proceed with caution and any such policy must be based on consultation between other people involved: project managers, archaeologists and conservators. It should never be the 'off-the-cuff' decision of the finder.

This book

This book is about how to prevent the deterioration of a find after you have located it. It is divided into chapters that discuss planning, processes of deterioration and preservation, what finds to expect and first-aid treatments and techniques, and includes a quick reference guide to storage. There are also notes on health hazards and how to proceed safely when dealing with chemicals and large finds.

What will you need

Normally you will need supplies of clean water, boxes, containers and some packaging materials. For delicate finds a refrigerator will be necessary. Many items could be recycled, salvaged, obtained second-hand or, with a little design ingenuity, built as required. Others, such as safety equipment or packaging materials, may have to be bought from hardware stores, garden centres or retail chemists, and on rare occasions, from specialist suppliers.

The materials covered

It is possible for any material to survive burial at an underwater site, even for thousands of years. Finds may be classified in different ways but in terms of first aid it is convenient to group them according to material type:

- organic materials (deriving from plants or animals, and including environmental remains)
- metals
- minerals, ceramics and glass
- composite finds (made from more than one material).

These are the classifications that have been used throughout this book.

2 Before you start

What to do when you locate a site

Archaeological sites provide unique opportunities for learning about the past. They contain a wealth of evidence that can be damaged in many ways, not only by the forces of nature but also by human actions. It is particularly unfortunate if those actions are unnecessary, and if sites are not exploited in a way that results in new knowledge about the past. All archaeological sites, even individual finds, are unique and non-replaceable mixtures of clues about life gone by. It is possible to collect such information and yet keep the find or site for future enjoyment and research.

It is very important to leave objects where they are found until specialist advice is sought. This will usually give the finds a better chance of surviving in the long term. Over the time that they are submerged or buried, materials reach a kind of equilibrium with their immediate environment. If this balance is upset, the object can suffer irreversible changes. Moreover, the disturbance may not be necessary because a great deal of information can be gained from survey and recording alone. Before any find is recovered the advantages and disadvantages of recovery must be carefully assessed and an informed judgement made.

Underwater archaeology has well established methods, which aim to ensure that the investigation, identification and interpretation of the site are undertaken to the highest standards. This may, or may not involve removal of finds. The archaeological discipline has developed techniques for maximising the return from the investigation and enables high quality data to be collected, which are then made available in a variety of forms, for example for education, museum display or academic research. However, in common with forensic science, archaeological investigation may only build up an adequate record of the site through painstaking attention to details, which, at first, may seem mundane or unimportant.

It may be that you or your team have already located an artefact or site. Perhaps you have discovered large, obtrusive finds, such as cannon or ship's timbers, or you may have chanced upon an individual item or cluster of stray finds, such as scattered pieces of pottery or small metal objects. It could be that a known site has recently become exposed by nearby coastal erosion or by constructional developments, or its specific location may just have been discovered after years of research. No matter what the circumstance of discovery there are certain legal procedures you must follow and agencies or organisations you must contact (see Appendix D for addresses).

Procedures

- Record the precise location of the site and leave finds in place.
- Keep the discovery secret and obtain expert archaeological advice.
- Conduct initial research to try to establish the identity and date of the site. In England, Scotland and Wales the national heritage bodies such as the Royal Commission on Historic Monuments (RCHM) may be able to help.
- Consult a museum or regional archaeologist for advice and guidance on whether there is an organisation likely to be interested in acquiring any of the finds.
- Seek advice from an archaeological conservator.
- If you are working in the UK the Archaeological Diving Unit (ADU) or the Nautical Archaeology Society (NAS) can give you further archaeological advice and, possibly, practical help. The ADU visits underwater sites thought to be of archaeological or historical interest in order to assess them. Other countries may have similar archaeological diving teams who could help. The NAS can advise on this, and arranges training courses in Britain and abroad. In addition, you may apply to the NAS for the Joan Du Plat Taylor Award to assist your research.
- In the UK, any marine object brought ashore must be reported by law to the Receiver of Wreck (HM Coastguard). Non-marine finds of an archaeological or historical nature may not be covered by maritime law in all countries, but should still be reported to a local museum or other archaeological or heritage body in order to alert them to the presence of the site. Sites found in England, Wales and Northern Ireland may fall within the Treasure Act 1996.
- If your site lies in a country outside the UK, investigate the requirements there. A museum, university or society specialising in maritime archaeology or history should be able to provide advice.

Marine finds in the UK

In many countries there is specific legislation to cover finds of archaeological or historical importance, although the original finders of the site could still become part of the archaeological team, and then closely involved in the survey and publication of the find. In the UK there are three relevant Acts of Parliament: the Protection of Wrecks Act 1975; the Protection of Military Remains Act 1986; and the Merchant Shipping Act 1894.

For a wreck to become protected the site must be found to be of archaeological, artistic or historical importance. It will then become designated under the terms of the Protection of Wrecks Act 1975. Unauthorised interference will then be prevented and only named divers will be allowed to dive on the site. If the site does not require protection, anyone will be free to dive on it. You would be advised, however, to learn as much as you can about the site before you begin diving.

You may discover you are not dealing with an ancient wreck, but with the remains of a military aircraft or vessel. If this is the case, the Protection of Military Remains Act 1986 will come into force, and any diving activities may be restricted. For further information contact the Royal Air Force, Innsworth (see Appendix D for addresses).

In the UK any marine finds you recover must be reported to the Receiver of Wreck, who will try to establish ownership. The law allows the true owner one year from the date of the report in which to claim the property back. If no legitimate claimant is forthcoming, for example if no descendant of an undisputed owner is found, the recovered property becomes unclaimed wreck and the Receiver of Wreck is required to dispose of it. This may be through sale, or the Receiver of Wreck may allow the finder to keep the material as a reward in lieu of salvage. The Coastguard Agency does try to avoid archaeological collections falling into private hands, and such objects are normally offered to a registered repository, preferably near the site.

Further information about UK legislation and how to report finds to the Receiver of Wreck or a museum is covered in *Museums and Maritime Archaeology* (Allen 1995). Pamphlets and guidance notes are also issued by the Receiver of Wreck. For information about techniques of underwater archaeology, read *Archaeology Underwater* (Dean *et al.* 1995) and join one of the NAS training courses.

See Plate 1 (colour section, p. i).

Developing a conservation strategy

Following consultation between all interested bodies it may be decided that finds must be recovered. You will then need to work with an archaeological conservator to develop an appropriate strategy. This involves further consultation between a range of specialists and organisations, such as heritage bodies, archaeological advisers, finds specialists, museum curators, analytical scientists, dating laboratories, the

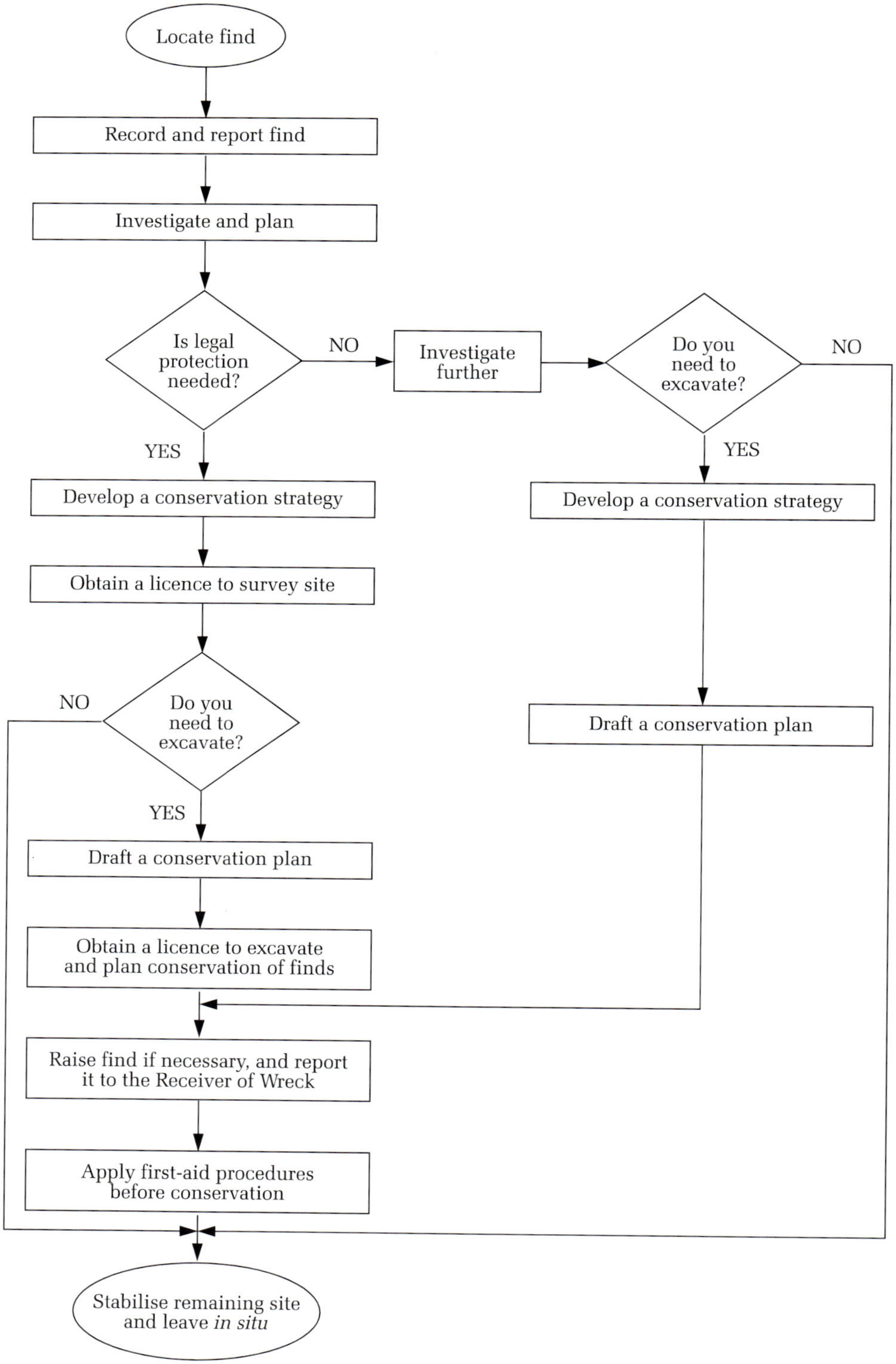

Figure 1 *Dealing with marine finds in the United Kingdom.*

Receiver of Wreck, ADU, sponsors, construction workers, and so on. You will need to draw up a costing of archaeological and conservation needs (both for first aid and for long-term conservation), negotiate a contract for conservation services and produce a project plan with clearly defined timescales, stages and deadlines.

The purpose of the conservation strategy is to plan the long-term future of the artefacts and to develop the main goals towards which you can work. You will need to establish a policy, covering:

- the exposure and further investigation of the site, bearing in mind the rate at which materials deteriorate
- the recovery of material and whether this can be justified in terms of current legislation, probable loss if left, the expense involved, and so on
- the subsequent housing or disposal of the finds and their long-term conservation prospects
- the publication of the finds in suitable journals, such as the *International Journal of Nautical Archaeology* (*IJNA*), published by NAS.

There is no justification for removing a find merely because it has been discovered. However, if after all options have been considered this is deemed necessary and in the best interests of the find, the site, its archaeology and the global heritage, and if sufficient funds are available to meet these needs and provide for conservation, the next stage is to formulate a conservation plan. Conservation can become a demanding and long-term undertaking.

The first-aid conservation plan

The purpose of the first-aid conservation plan is to ensure that all practical preparations for initial conservation have been made, and that the recovery operation can run smoothly. For this you will need to establish:

- a list of predicted finds and materials from which they are made
- a policy on backfilling or conservation *in situ*
- arrangements for the long-term housing of the finds
- arrangements for conservation and a contract with a conservation laboratory
- a conservation budget and how this will be financed
- arrangements for scientific dating or analysis of finds and which procedures to take
- arrangements for X-ray and conventional photography
- the priority of the finds, putting those that need urgent treatment ahead of others
- arrangements for transportation of finds to the first-aid workshop

- procedures for recording first-aid treatments
- the treatment, storage and packaging of finds
- arrangements for transportation and delivery to the conservation laboratory.

Appoint a supervisor to take responsibility for the first-aid conservation plan. This could be you. Duties will include:

- taking charge of the first-aid budget
- supervision of the planning and implementation of the project's conservation strategy
- supervision of first-aid assistants and helpers
- assembling and cleaning storage and packing materials and other equipment
- acquiring any necessary storage chemicals and making up the solutions
- preparing labels and maintaining other conservation documentation
- close involvement in any decision to raise a find (whether to raise it and if so, when)
- responsibility for the first-aid treatment of finds following recovery
- responsibility for the security of finds receiving treatment and in storage
- responsibility for safety when using chemicals and in their storage and disposal.

Prioritising treatment

Underwater excavations can yield a vast amount of material, and in particular organic finds. In a large excavation this material may seem to arrive incessantly, and can overwhelm a small, first-aid workshop. What must be avoided is a 'last-in first-out' arrangement,where the most recently arrived finds are placed at the top of a holding bath and are treated ahead of others that have been languishing at the bottom for some time. Just as bad is the situation where the first-aid supervisor does not know the nature of the finds until they reach their turn in the queue, perhaps days or even weeks after they have been recovered. It is essential that a scheme be devised whereby finds requiring urgent attention are identified and treated accordingly.

The finds at greatest risk are perishable items such as charts, documents, paper and card. These can be expected to deteriorate within minutes of exposure to light or atmospheric conditions. Urgent attention is therefore critical.

Finds are sometimes too large or bulky to be totally submerged in storage tanks on site. Such finds may include large pieces of ironwork, cannon and timbers. Every effort must be made to keep them totally submerged in holding baths after they have been recovered, but sometimes this cannot be achieved. Instead, they must be wrapped and packed to protect them from drying and monitored hourly until suitable storage containers can be found.

The next category includes finds that will probably be stable for up to a day, if kept totally submerged in holding baths and out of the sun. These include textiles, fibrous materials, leather and composites. Again, they will need careful monitoring, and must receive further attention before the end of the day.

Other finds may be stable for up to several days if stored submerged in baths of clean water. Examples include small items of wood or lead. Again, these finds must be totally submerged and monitored, and must receive attention before the end of a week.

Some finds will probably be stable for longer periods. These generally include metals, bones, glass, pottery, stone and some samples required for analysis or dating. They will, however, need checking daily for signs of water discolouration or evaporation. Clean tap water may be used to replenish water levels.

Chapter 3 describes how finds deteriorate and suggests how this can be prevented.

3 How finds deteriorate

Processes of deterioration

In the right conditions even the most vulnerable of finds can survive for thousands of years under water. Deterioration proceeds very quickly at first, but then slows down and may virtually stop. Such a point is reached when the 'energy' needed to alter a find is greater than the 'force' exerted by the environment. An equilibrium between the find and the environment is established. This state of equilibrium is upset when new forces are introduced, which is generally whenever the environment is disturbed. When this happens deterioration processes may proceed alarmingly quickly, and continue until either equilibrium is re-established, or the find is destroyed. First-aid measures are an attempt to prevent this.

When is a find vulnerable?

A find becomes vulnerable to deterioration from the moment of discovery, even if it is never raised. New forces, caused simply by exposing the find as it is being excavated, make it prone to attack. As the excavation progresses the find may be damaged further as it loses the physical protection afforded by the burial deposit; it could be broken, damaged, eaten, trodden on or washed away. Vulnerable during transportation to the surface, when it reaches the top it is at even greater risk. It then loses the buoyant support of the water and experiences a dramatic increase in weight. It may crack or break as a result. Out of the water, it is vulnerable to changes in the environment: it is exposed to a rich supply of oxygen in the air; a warm, breezy atmosphere may cause it to dry out, even if it is only exposed for a moment; it may be attacked by increased activity of micro-organisms, algae and fungi; and it might be crushed beneath the weight of a heavier object carelessly placed on top of it. Physical, chemical and biological threats combine to put a newly discovered find at risk.

See Plate 2 (colour section, p. i)

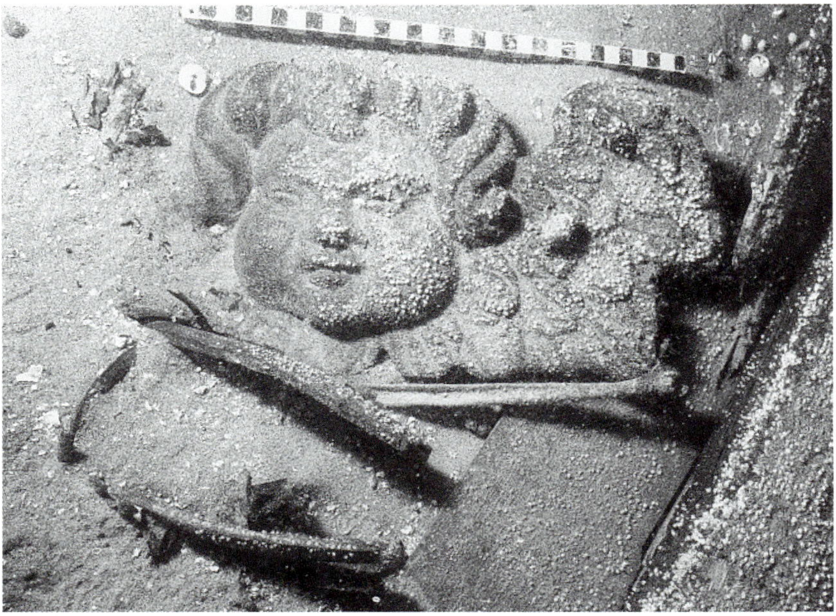

An organic deposit exposed on the Duart Point wreck in 1992. Elements of the ship structure appear on the right, while the partially exposed wooden cherub shows barnacle infestation indicative of progressive exposure from the upper right. In the centre foreground is a small stave-built vessel, its top elements recently removed by exposure, while between it and the cherub is a human ulna. The barnacle infestation of the cherub has occurred recently. (Archaeological Diving Unit)

Physical damage or loss

Physical damage may be caused by water currents, plant and animal life, incorrect handling or accidental drying. Careless loss can occur if a find is dropped while being transported to the surface, discarded with debris, misplaced or simply given the wrong identification label. The find might also be stolen. Upon drying, surface tensions cause fibrous or cellular structures to collapse, and the forces of salts crystallising as water evaporates may cause surfaces to flake away.

Early signs of physical damage include the appearance of worn, smooth surfaces, ridges and other marks and indentations. Embrittlement, surface cracking and distortions are caused by drying. Salt crystallisation is characterised by powdery, white stains and the flaking or dislodging of surface layers.

Physical damage can be prevented by careful handling with close attention being given to packaging, support and measures to prevent drying. Exposure to water currents or the effects of destructive animal life can be minimised by backfilling and the use of sandbags or underwater deposits to cover the site after excavation.

Chemical damage

Metals are most at risk of chemical damage, but concretions and glass are also vulnerable. Chemical action may also cause the oxidation or alteration of other non-metallic substances. Chemical damage will occur when finds are exposed to higher concentrations of oxygen, different levels of salinity, acidity or alkalinity (pH) or to increased temperatures.

Signs to look for are the find becoming warm or releasing bubbles – especially in the case of iron. Finds may also change colour, or rusty stains may appear on the object itself, in its storage solution or on its wrappings. Eventually cracks may appear and fragments of the find will fall away. The process is irreversible, and if allowed to continue unchecked the find will disintegrate completely.

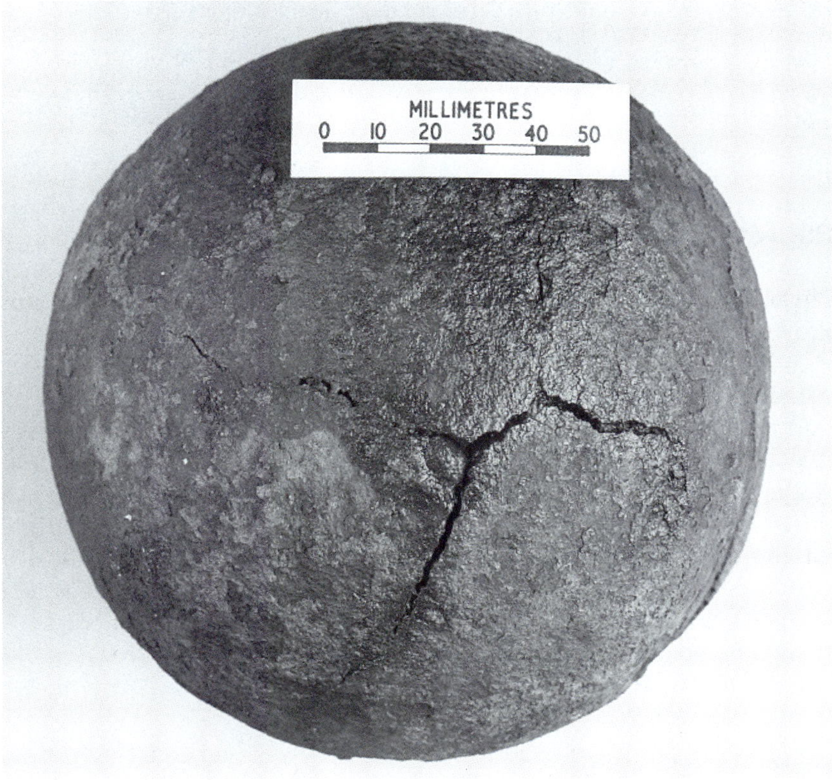

A cast iron cannon ball showing signs of falling apart. (B. Harris)

Chemical damage can be reduced by lowering temperatures, adjusting pH levels or removing aggressive reagents such as oxygen and dissolved salts. In extreme cases, the introduction of a chemical inhibitor may be required.

Biological decay

Biological decay (where the material is consumed by a living organism) can occur to any substance that is organic in nature (coming from a plant or animal source), such as wood, leather, paper, textiles, fibres, foodstuffs, and so on. It may be caused by micro-organisms (bacteria, slime moulds, microfungi), algal growth, higher moulds and fungi, and animals, such as insects or marine borers. A find suffering biological decay may be attacked at a microscopic or higher level. If left unchecked, it will result in destruction.

In the early stages biological decay can be difficult to detect without close examination but recognisable signs include sliminess and the appearance of black or brightly coloured stains, either on the surface of the storage solution or the finds. Green algal blooms and threads of fungal hyphae, or, in extreme cases, fungal fruiting bodies (mushrooms), should also sound the alarm. Animal activity is usually detected by the presence of frass (sawdust left behind by wood-boring animals), droppings, tooth or claw marks, bore holes or the flight holes of adult insects.

Methods of controlling biological damage include *in situ* techniques such as backfilling and minimising exposure during excavation. Following the recovery of finds biological activity can best be controlled by keeping material chilled and in darkened conditions. Storage in flowing water or water that is regularly changed may also help to control growths.

Biocides should be avoided at all costs: they have unknown additives and may react with some finds. They also introduce health risks and may be poisonous; many can be absorbed through the skin, even when diluted in solution. They are even more dangerous in concentrated or powder form and may cause skin or lung irritation and chemical burns, and the disposal of waste or concentrated biocides could have harmful effects on the environment. Only on very rare occasions will the use of biocides be necessary; for example in warm climates where cool temperatures and flowing water are not an option. In such cases the conservation laboratory engaged to treat the finds must be consulted for specific advice.

In the past some laboratories adopted freezing as a method of long-term storage, especially when they were confronted with large amounts of vulnerable material or sensitive finds such as waterlogged books or archival works on paper. Now, with the benefit of hindsight, conservators are more cautious. They have found that in certain cases ice crystals within the fabric of the find caused damage to the cellular structure and made subsequent treatment more difficult. Freezing is now usually only acceptable as part of a conservation programme for wood and leather that have been pretreated to remove some of the water, and as a direct precursor to freeze-drying. Freezing finds as a first-aid measure is no longer advisable.

First-aid treatment

In applying first-aid treatment, the aim is to prevent physical damage, chemical alteration and biological decay. By far the best option is to leave finds *in situ,* where the natural environment may continue to preserve them. However, if the find or site is threatened in some way, recovery may be necessary. Guidance from an archaeological conservator is essential, but it will help if you have an understanding of the behaviour and characteristics of each type of find. This involves the ability to recognise the find's main material and understand the ways in which it may deteriorate. Knowledge of the archaeological or dating potential of the find and an appreciation of how all this might affect recording and subsequent treatment are also important, and the long-term conservation prospects and incurred costs must also be considered. All this is discussed in Part 2.

II

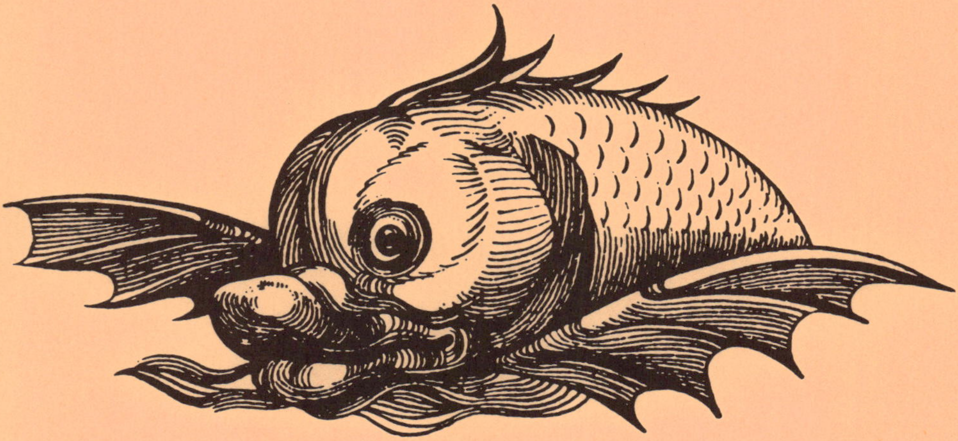

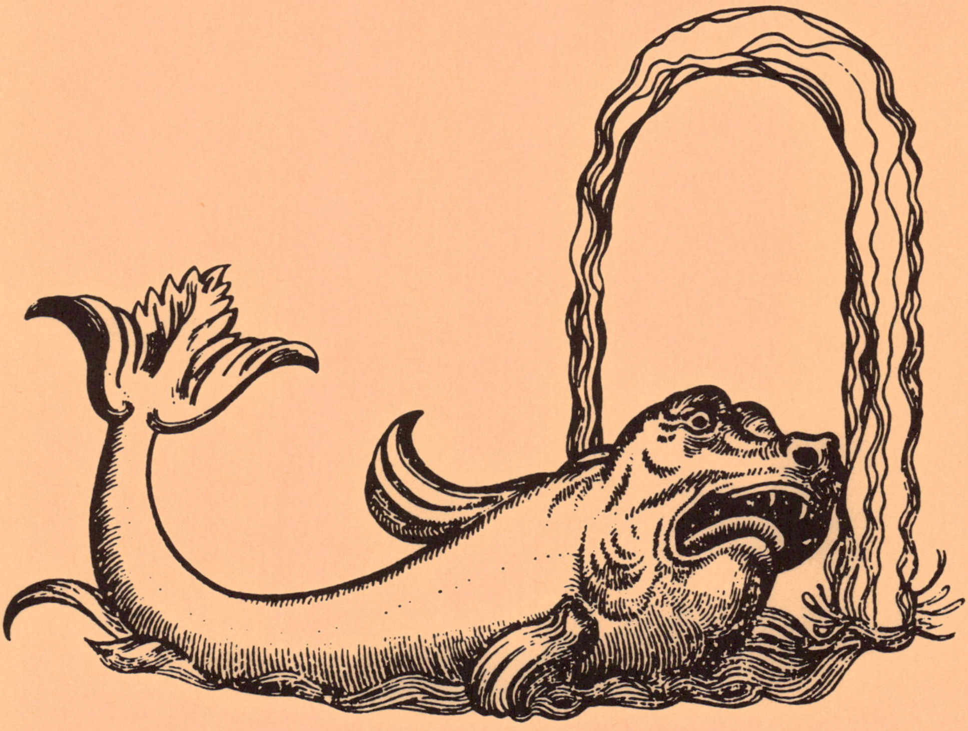

Materials, objects and finds

Before you undertake any first-aid treatment it is important to understand a little about the materials you are treating. This is important because some materials may respond well to one type of treatment while others will not and if a find has potential for scientific analysis or dating, special treatment (or no treatment at all) might be required. The exact nature of the substance is often difficult to determine, although identification of the artefact might provide a clue.

Knowing the particular risks a find might be subject to and how quickly it can be expected to change will enable you to prioritise treatments and arrange first-aid processing to make best use of time and resources. In the following chapters, finds are classified according to the type of materials from which they are likely to be composed, with background information about them. Detailed descriptions of first-aid treatments are given in Part 3.

4 Organic materials

Introduction

Definition

'Organic material' is the generic term given to materials or substances that originally came from a living source. It takes the form of remains of the living organism itself (bones, skeletons and insect cases, bark, wood, leaves, seeds and grains) or their waste products, artefacts made from animal substances or plant materials (for example scrimshaw carvings, ship hulls or wattle panelling) or new substances that have been manufactured or extracted (leather, parchment, textiles and foodstuffs).

Organic materials from underwater sites have a special significance because finds rarely come from land archaeological sites in such good condition. Moreover, the information they give can increase our knowledge of a host of subjects (diet, fashion, construction, trade, leisure activities and weaponry), as well as add to the ecological record of the time. Organic material can also be used for scientific dating.

Survival

Organic materials are generally found only in conditions that are free from oxygen: in anaerobic sediments; in anoxic lakes or waters; and inside sealed bottles or containers. Their survival is largely dependent upon a lack of oxygen, and when this changes, for example after excavation, organic materials can suffer (see p. 18).

Scientific dating of organic material

Radiocarbon dating

By their very nature, organic materials consist of high amounts of carbon, some of it in the form of radiocarbon (C^{14}), assimilated from the atmosphere when the plant or animal was living. This radiocarbon decays at a known rate and by measuring the amount that now remains, the approximate date of death of the organism can be established. Wood and bone are particularly suitable for radiocarbon dating, but unless steps are taken to protect them they may become contaminated by modern material, making any dating invalid. To prevent this, material selected for radiocarbon dating should be carefully packed in an inert material (polythene bags or boxes are suitable) and stored totally immersed in chilled, clean water, free from disinfectants, biocides or other chemicals. Smoking in the vicinity of samples will also affect the results, and must be banned. For specific advice, before you start excavating, you must contact the radiocarbon dating laboratory that will be dealing with the finds.

Dendrochronology

Another technique used for dating, this time specific to wood, is dendrochronology. The width of growth rings in timber differs from year to year depending upon prevailing climatic conditions: in dry summers the tree lays down wood slowly and the growth rings are thinner than in wetter periods. The resultant pattern of tree rings can be matched to an established sequence of tree-ring patterns now extending over many centuries. By this method a date range for samples of timber can be found. Again the dating laboratory will give advice on the precise conditions required for storage, but in any event the wood must never be allowed to dry out, as this will cause the tree-ring pattern to distort.

Full conservation treatment

Conservators treat organic finds from underwater sites by a variety of methods. The most common are impregnation with polyethylene glycol (PEG, a water-soluble wax), freeze-drying and drying through solvents.

SUMMARY

Organic Finds

Organic finds are very unstable and must be protected from:

- unnecessary exposure to new conditions underwater
- stresses and strains during lifting, recovery and transportation
- accidental drying following recovery, and during recording, photography, examination and cleaning
- degradation and attack by bacteria, algae, fungi and insects, during both treatment and storage.

Each of these processes can be lengthy and expensive, and involves specialist expertise.

See Plates 3 and 4 (colour section, p. ii)

The preservation of organic finds, and type of first-aid treatment, are often dependent upon their constituent materials. These can be classed as follows:

- timber and wood
- skin and gut products
- skeletal material and shell
- keratin-based finds (tortoiseshell, horn, whalebone)
- stems, fibres, paper, hair and wool
- solid foodstuffs (vegetable) and environmental material
- liquid and semi-liquid (fatty/waxy) foodstuffs and preparations
- resinous and mineral substances of organic origin.

Timber and wood

Typical materials

Timber, wood, bark, cork, twigs.

Typical finds

Small finds Personal items, gaming equipment, buttons; tools, instruments and equipment; small structural remains; corks from bottles and other containers; bowls, boxes and jars; handles of brushes, tools, knives and firearms; brooms.

Large finds Ships' timbers, furniture, fittings, figureheads and other types of accoutrement; gun carriages; chests, barrels; remains of settlements and dwellings such as stakes, posts, beams and wattle panels.

See Plates 5 and 6 (colour section, p. iii)

Composition and stability

Wood cells comprise two main substances: lignin and cellulose. Lignin, the woody, strength-giving component, accounts for the deceptively sturdy condition of some types of decayed wood. Provided that oxygen is restricted lignin is relatively indestructible. Not so the other component, cellulose, which is much more easily degraded. Thus finds may appear to be sound and robust, while in reality they are degraded and weak, all the cellulose having been consumed and the cells waterlogged. In this condition, wood needs protecting from accidental drying,

SUMMARY OF RISKS

Wood

Newly uncovered wood will normally be soft and fragile. Do not be deceived if it appears to be sound.

Wood must be protected from:

- unnecessary exposure to new conditions underwater
- stresses and strains during lifting and recovery
- accidental drying, even for a moment
- degradation and attack by bacteria, algae, fungi and insects, during or following storage and conservation.

physical damage and erosion, and biological attack, both before recovery and while in store. Waterlogged wood is very heavy and, following recovery, may be too heavy to support its own weight. Support for large timbers is therefore essential.

How wood deteriorates following discovery

Wood is generally dependent on an anaerobic environment for its stability. It is therefore vital to keep newly discovered wood exposed for the shortest possible time. Within the course of a season's excavation the surface of exposed wood can be worn away by water movements or, in marine environments, by the activity of creatures such as crabs, lobsters and barnacles. Workers all over the world are now recognising the extent to which wood can suffer and the far-reaching effects exposure can have (Guthrie *et al.* 1994).

Marine wood is also prone to attack by wood-boring organisms, such as the gribble (*Limnoria* spp.) – the marine cousin of the woodlouse – and shipworm (*Teredo* spp.), a mollusc. These creatures enthusiastically colonise newly exposed wood in most places where levels of oxygen or salinity are not too low; sites in fresh, brackish or anoxic waters will therefore be safe. Their activity can often be observed on the timber supports of piers exposed at low tide. Gribbles tunnel through the wood, eating it away and leaving it riddled with holes like woodworm. The channels of shipworms are much wider and are lined with the secreted shell of the *Teredo*. Wood that has suffered extensive shipworm attack may easily snap and have the appearance of an opened packet of cigarettes.

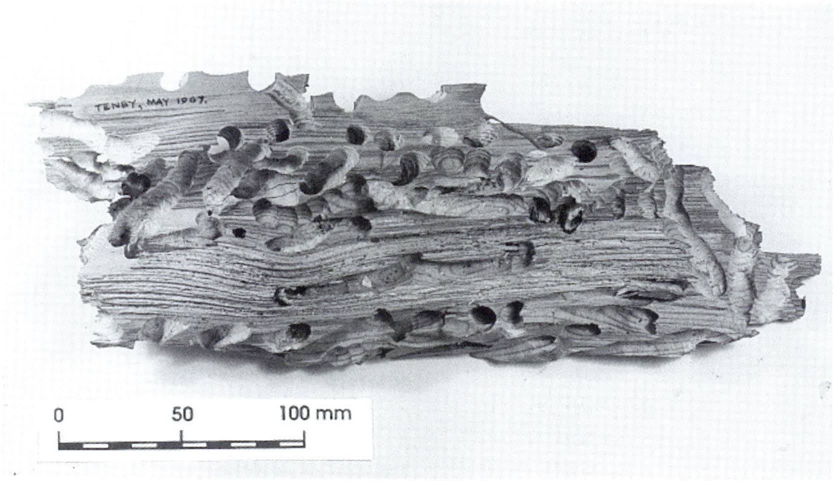

Wood that has been attacked by shipworm. (W. Robinson)

On a microscopic level, marine and other types of wood will be damaged by the growth of algae and wood-destroying bacteria or fungi that flourish in any oxygen-rich environment.

Wood will also be damaged by drying. The cellular structure of the wood is weakened during burial and waterlogging occurs. If the wood begins to dry, surface tensions pull the walls of the cells together and cause them to collapse. This results in shrinkage and distortion. The process can start within moments of exposure to drying conditions, and is irreversible.

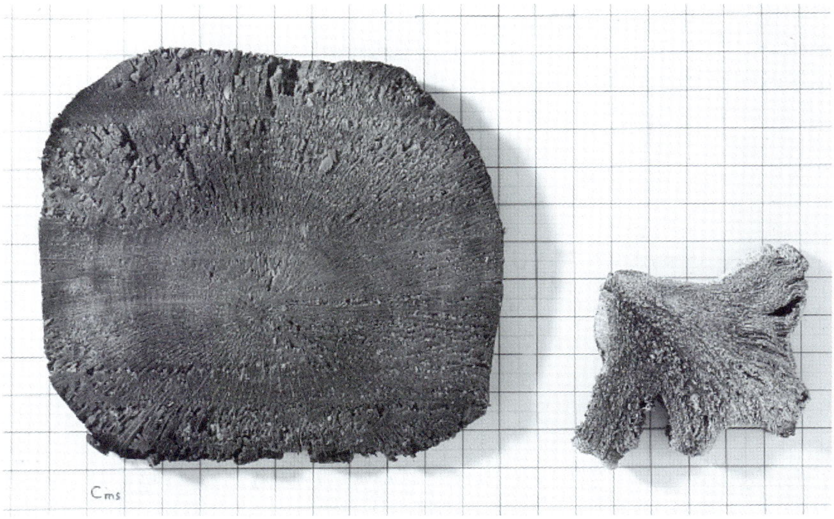

Samples of Douglas Fir showing the effects of drying. (National Maritime Museum)

Full conservation treatment

Before wood undergoes conservation, it is given a thorough analysis and expert examination to identify the species and determine the water content. Once this has been done, the conservator can choose from several methods of conservation. The most widely used are those based on impregnation with PEGs, applied either by total immersion or by spraying, perhaps followed by freeze-drying or drying without heat, in the air. These treatments, although successful when under the control of a qualified conservator, can be lengthy (particularly in the case of ships' timbers) and expensive. One estimate for conserving a wooden pulley block, taking five conservator days, has been placed at £545: another, for conserving just a third of a prehistoric wattle panel from a beach in the northeast of England, has been put at £27,000 (Allen 1995).

Although expensive, treatments involving PEG have been used extensively over the past four decades. PEG was first employed on a grand scale for the Swedish warship *Wasa* in Stockholm and then on the medieval cog of Bremen, West Germany. In the UK, the hull of the *Mary Rose* is currently being sprayed continuously with PEG solutions. The spray system, introduced in 1994, includes over 500 metres of pipework and 320 stainless steel nozzles. The process is expected to take decades to complete and needs a full conservation unit to supervise and monitor it. The cost of the total operation will run into millions of pounds.

See Plate 7 (colour section, p. iv)

There have been some reports of wood being allowed to 'slow-dry' in normal conditions, and these might appeal as a cheap and easy method of wet wood conservation. But these methods can spell disaster if they are not monitored very carefully and should never be attempted by the non-specialist. Before any such treatment begins there must be a thorough and detailed examination by a wood expert in order to identify the wood species, the extent of deterioration and the water content. Based on the results the wood conservator will be able to decide whether slow drying is a feasible option, and if so, what is to be the optimum rate and length of time. Slow drying is never a simple answer; if not properly managed it can lead to total disaster.

A summary of first-aid treatments

Before being recovered

Throughout the excavation, keep wooden finds exposed for the minimum amount of time to avoid erosion and damage, and at the end of the season, backfilling or covering with sandbags might be appropriate. Before recovery, pack wooden finds carefully and be sure to give them good support. Aim to construct a support to take the weight of the find, that can also be used to manoeuvre it.

Initial storage/cleaning

Wooden finds must be kept wet: totally immersed; sprayed continuously; or covered in water-saturated coverings with an overlay of heavy duty polythene, polyvinyl chloride sheeting (PVC) or tarpaulin.

Cleaning must only be done under the supervision of a conservator. It may be possible to remove loose debris and detritus by gentle spraying, but avoid brushing, as this will wear away any softened components and may inadvertently remove evidence of painting, gilding, decoration, rivets, and so on. Stop spraying immediately if you find anything of this nature.

Recording (drawing)

Before large wooden finds are packed for long-term storage they should be photographed and drawn. Note on your drawing any markings and using the conventions described by Clarke *et al.* (1993). It is during the recording process that wooden finds may accidentally dry out. Take steps to prevent this, for example by spraying the find at short, regular intervals.

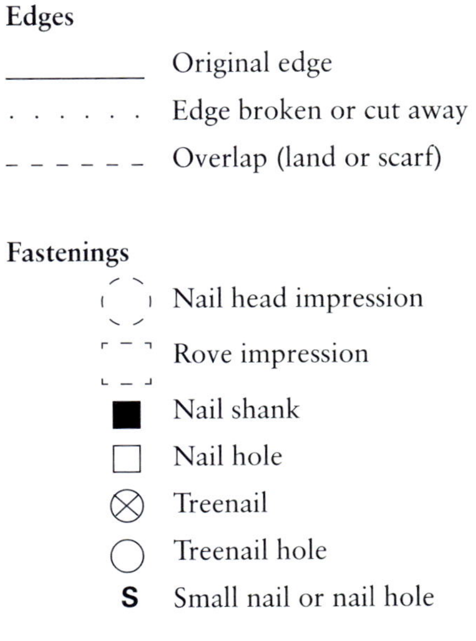

Figure 2 *Drawing conventions for recording timbers (after Clarke* et al. *1993).*

FIRST-AID SUMMARY

Wood

Backfilling

- Protect timbers that are not being raised by covering them with sandbags or by some other means.

Excavated finds

- Always make sure the find has sufficient support and padding.
- Manipulate the support, not the find.
- Keep finds wet at all times, either by total immersion in running water or by covering them with hessian, towelling or some other absorbent material and then by spraying or drenching with cold water.
- Cover the find with plastic sheeting or tarpaulin to reduce evaporation rates.

Cleaning

- CAUTION: over-zealous cleaning will obliterate archaeological evidence.
- Use only gentle spraying and remove only loose silt and debris. Avoid brushing which may damage softened surfaces, and do not dislodge any adherent material.

Storage (wet)

- Keep finds in darkened conditions and at chilled temperatures below 4°C. Running water is best, but chilled, still water can be used. It should be changed whenever biological growths are detected.
- Seal finds in water-tight boxes or lined crates. First pad the finds carefully with polyether or polythene foam, or polythene bubble-pack, to stop them being damaged.
- If they are too large to be stored covered in water and kept chilled, keep finds damp and seal them in layers of plastic or metallised polythene tubing. Keep them free from insect attack and if possible in darkened conditions.
- Do not freeze this type of find.

Freezing

Archaeologists and conservators advise against freezing wood. A frozen find is difficult to draw or record, and the process of freezing itself may cause damage within the cells.

Drying

Waterlogged wood should never be dried before conservation as this will result in shrinkage and distortion.

Long-term storage

Finds made of wood must be kept totally immersed in clean water. If this is not possible protect the wood by covering it in water-saturated wrapping and sealing it between layers of polythene. Monitor the wood weekly to check that water is not evaporating.

Skin and gut products

Typical materials

Rawhide and furs, tanned leather, vellum, parchment, catgut, sinew.

Typical finds

Charts, documents and book-bindings; clothing and footwear; bags, bottles, containers and cases; equipment, tools and instruments; binding threads, thongs and cords.

Well preserved soft tissue will not normally survive in underwater conditions so any naturally preserved bodies, like those found desiccated in sand, frozen in ice or tanned naturally in peat-bogs, are unlikely to be found. However, excavators should be prepared for soft tissue remains in association with items of leather clothing or footwear, or even preserved within the cavities of skulls.

See Plates 8 and 9 (colour section, p. iv)

Composition and stability

Skin and gut products derive from the fibrous protein collagen and this generally survives well in oxygen-free conditions. Leather, which has had its resistance to water and biological attack increased by tanning processes, can survive particularly well, although the natural oils and any associated bulking materials may have been lost. When this is the case, the leather will become brittle as it dries and may tend to split in a lateral direction. Its natural colour will also have been lost and any hair or fur will no longer be fixed. If components of these skin and gut products have further reacted with the water to become hydrolysed, their surfaces will be soft and perhaps soapy and even paste-like. There will be points of weakness along any folds or creases, or where the material is adhering to an underlying substance such as brass or wood.

'Catgut' is a material made from sheep's intestines and responds to underwater burial in much the same way as leather.

Full conservation treatment

Skin and gut products may be treated using a variety of methods owing to the varying state in which these materials will be found, the processes involved in their manufacture and the different uses to which they were put. Nevertheless, in professional hands conservation treatments often meet with some success, some examples being restored to their natural colour and flexibility. However, it is uncertain whether the original dimensions of the finds can ever be established, in so far as these are known. Methods of conservation include replacing water with PEG, oils or tannins, drying through solvents or water repellents, and freeze-drying. Complications arise in the case of decorated or composite finds.

A summary of first-aid treatments

Examination of archival material by infra-red (IR) photography or ultraviolet (UV) light

In the lucky event of archival material being found (parchment or vellum charts, documents, book-bindings), watch out for remains of ink, dyes or writing and take great care to protect them. Such evidence is immensely important, yet so easily destroyed merely by exposure to light. If there is any possibility that you may have such a find, refrain from attempting to clean it, and keep it chilled and in darkened conditions. Have the find photographed by a specialist on IR film, as this might reveal further evidence of decoration or writing.

Some inks and dyes will also show up under an UV light, but this is a technique best left to a qualified conservator or archivist. There are health risks involved, as well as the possibility that such examination may itself cause evidence to fade.

Preliminary examination and recording

Before treating these finds it is important to give them a thorough and detailed examination, taking note of the following:

WARNING – URGENT ATTENTION REQUIRED

Inks, dyes, writing found on charts, documents or leather? You may have discovered something of utmost importance, but something that is highly unstable.

If you suspect that writing or ink or pigmentation is present:

- immediately consult a conservator or specialist archivist
- keep the find in the dark
- do not clean the find – try to keep it covered in its burial deposit
- do not expose the find to biocides or to any other chemicals
- do not expose the find to light of any kind, and especially not photofloods
- investigate the possibility of having the find photographed in IR light

Remember – prompt action is essential.

- stitching, stitch or eyelet holes
- inks and dyes
- branded marks
- evidence of wear
- size and dimensions
- type of animal hide (you may need a reference book)
- the presence of human or environmental remains
- textiles imprints or remains
- contents of containers or bottles
- pigmentation or gilding.

If the find is strong enough arrange it on a supporting surface (for example, plastic sheet or synthetic netting) and, if flat, record the dimensions by tracing over the shape on to plastic film (eg Melinex) with a good quality, permanent, waterproof marker (Artline or Staedler manufacture suitable pens). It is important to record the dimensions of the find as soon as possible following recovery, and to keep the finds wet at all times during the recording process.

Initial storage and cleaning

Always keep skin and gut finds in cool or chilled conditions and out of bright light – even during recording processes. If cleaning is being carried out (only under conservation supervision), keep exposure times to a minimum and use gentle spraying with chilled water. Always place the find on a support – the support can then be manœuvred instead of the find. Remove loose deposits by brushing gently with a soft bristled paint brush or, better, with a gentle stream or spray of chilled water. This must be done very carefully under expert supervision. If you suspect the presence of any pigmentation, inks, gilding, dyes, paint or environmental material, cleaning should stop and the find should immediately be returned to dark and chilled storage.

Drying

Do not allow any find in this category to dry, even for a moment.

Freezing

It is not advisable to freeze skin and gut finds.

Long-term storage

Store skin and gut finds totally immersed in fresh or tap water. If the find is too large for a container, seal it in polythene and keep it refrigerated. Always remember to check every week for evaporation.

FIRST-AID SUMMARY

Skin and gut products

These materials are vulnerable and need prompt attention.

- Immobilise finds before recovery and keep fragments from being washed away by currents.
- Keep finds wet and chilled at all times and in darkened conditions.
- Never allow finds to dry out.
- Do not freeze these finds.

Skeletal material

Typical materials

Bone, ivory, tooth, tusk, antler, shell, coral. (For whalebone, tortoise shell, horn, and so on, see the section on keratin based materials, p. 39.)

Typical finds

Human/animal remains; carvings and models; pins, combs, buttons, boxes and containers; cargo items; jewellery, amulets and pendants; tools, weapons, instruments or their handles; inlay; shell lantern lights, mother of pearl, abalone and inlays of these on other objects.

See Plate 10 (colour section p. v)

Composition and stability

Skeletal materials are a combination of animal protein and inorganic substances. The main components of antler and bone are primarily hydroxyapatite and calcium phosphate. Shell is similar, being protein and calcium carbonate, whereas ivory and tooth are composed of dentine, with the dentine of tooth being coated in enamel. It is sometimes difficult to differentiate between these types of finds but they can usually be distinguished by examining their cellular structures. Bone tends to be relatively porous, 'spongy' and often fibrous, whereas elephant ivory can sometimes be distinguished by a characteristic intersecting arrangement of concentric arcs. Tooth may be ridged.

Skeletal materials, especially tooth, shell and ivory, are at risk through drying, which may cause them to split, laminate, crack or distort. It is sometimes possible to dry any animal bones needed mainly for identification or archaeological study, but you must act only on the advice of the bone specialist engaged to deal with them.

How skeletal material deteriorates

The preservation of skeletal material is usually dependent on anaerobic, alkaline conditions (as found in marine deposits and at the bottom of some lakes). They become softened in acidic lake deposits, but in alkaline and carbonate-rich waters calcification starts to take place, and in the long term this benefits the preservation processes.

Dating and archaeological importance

Bone and ivory may be suitable for radiocarbon dating (see p. 25 for details of radiocarbon dating). It is important to avoid cross-contamination with similar material or with modern substances such as dust, cigarette ash, biocides and organic chemicals.

A study of these materials by a bone specialist can also provide information about the individual's sex, stature and age at death (perhaps even leading to clues about their identity), as well as details of health, diet and disease, or, in the case of animals, information about the species, trends in animal husbandry and methods of butchery.

Full conservation treatment

The treatment of skeletal material can be very complex, as manufactured artefacts are often found in association with other material, for example the bone handle of an iron knife or a bodkin case full of needles. For unworked animal bones, conservators and bone specialists may sometimes advise little more than desalination and drying. Even after conservation these finds remain sensitive to changes in temperature and relative humidity and must be stored in controlled conditions.

SUMMARY

Skeletal material – Bone, ivory, tooth

Keep finds wet

- Seal in polythene bags or boxes and keep finds in chilled, darkened conditions. Change the storage water if biological growths occur.

Samples for analysis or dating

- Avoid any risk of cross-contamination. Never use biocides and ban smoking. Obtain further advice from the dating laboratory.

Composite finds

- See Appendix A for storage details.

A summary of first-aid treatments

Bones required for radiocarbon dating

Do not treat these finds in any way other than by storing them immersed in clean water, keep in chilled conditions and in the dark. Prevent contamination from modern organic substances and cigarette smoke or ash. The dating laboratory concerned will give you more specific advice on storage and packaging.

Cleaning

Work only under the supervision of a qualified conservator. Finds not needed for radiocarbon dating may be gently cleaned by removing loose debris with a soft brush or by spraying. Watch out for evidence of painting, gilding, decoration, rivets, and so on, and stop if you find any. Special care is needed with teeth still held in jawbones, which will probably be loose.

Desalination

This must only be undertaken under the supervision of a conservator who will be able to determine by scientific methods when the process is complete.

Drying

Skeletal material must never be dried as part of its first-aid treatment.

Long-term storage

Wet finds should be stored totally immersed in clean water or sealed in polythene. Chilled, darkened conditions are required to eliminate biological degradation. If biological activity is noted the storage water must be changed. Do not use biocides.

Keratin-based finds

Typical materials

Baleen (whalebone), snake-skin, horn, feather, claw, hoof, tortoiseshell. Hair, wool and bristle are also materials based on keratin, but see the section on fibres for their treatment (p. 40).

Typical finds

Carvings and scrimshaw, drinking horns, amulets, combs, inlays, quills.

Composition and stability

Keratin-based finds are made from the hard protein, keratin. They are generally resistant in favourable conditions but are liable to crack or split when they dry.

Full conservation treatment

Keratin-based finds are likely to be part of composite items so conservation will be complex. They usually respond well to freeze-drying but after treatment will still require storage or display conditions which are strictly controlled in terms of constant, low temperatures and relative humidity set to a constant level. They also need to be protected from visible and UV light.

SUMMARY

Horn, baleen, tortoiseshell, quill, feather, hoof, claw

- Keep finds wet, sealed in polythene bags or boxes, store at chilled temperatures and keep in darkened conditions. If biological growths occur, change the storage solution.

A summary of first-aid treatments

Initial storage and cleaning

Keep keratin-based finds wet, and in the dark. Under the supervision of a qualified conservator you may attempt to remove soft debris and detritus by gentle spraying.

Drying

Do not attempt to dry these finds.

Long-term storage

Store keratin-based finds by totally immersing them in water, or packing and sealing them in polythene bags or wrappings. Keep them in chilled, darkened conditions and replace the storage water if biological growths occur. Monitor storage conditions regularly.

Fibres, stems, hair, wool and paper

Typical materials

Cotton; linen, hemp, jute; grasses, reeds, sedges; hair, wool, kemp, silk, rhino horn.

Typical finds

These finds are very vulnerable to decay and can only survive in special circumstances, although cordage, rigging and sailcloth are usually found in bulk. Complete survival is very unusual at non-marine sites, but small fragments of material sometimes survive.

Typical finds include: sacks, bags, textiles, clothing and trimmings; rugs, carpets and wall hangings; matting and basketry; fishing nets, rope, cordage, rigging and sailcloth; satin, velvet, wadding and felt;

knitting, weaving, tapestry, embroidery and appliqué work; metal-bound threads; paper, card and documents.

See Plate 11 (colour section, p. vi)

Archaeological significance

These finds are common on marine sites, and particularly on wrecks, but they have been frequently overlooked in the past. The information they can convey is limited only by the number of analytical resources applied to them. They may be of great archival importance and often hold information about art, style and fashion.

Composition and stability

In normal, wet or damp conditions, fibres, stems, hair, wool and paper rot very quickly and it is surprising that any survive at all. Plant derivatives, and particularly cotton, contain large quantitites of cellulose, which degrades very quickly. The lignin content of the bast (stem) fibres of linen, hemp and jute make them a little more resistant, as does silica in grasses, reeds and sedges. Paper and card, which are made from cellulose fibres held together by a size, are extremely unstable and are only found in exceptional circumstances.

Animal fibres (wool, bristle and silk) are protein-based and are generally more resistant to decay. Excellent examples of fine knitting were found at the medieval crannog site at Llangorse Lake, Wales. Nevertheless, all these materials are highly unstable and very soft and can easily be damaged. They require urgent attention.

See Plates 12, 13, 14 and 15 (colour section, pp. vi–vii)

How they deteriorate

Where oxygen is present, even in small amounts, fragile items like these will decay within a matter of days; if it is excluded right from the start, they may well survive. These finds will therefore normally be found only in special circumstances, such as in places that have been sealed in some way, perhaps under a compact layer of clay or silt, or inside wooden or metal boxes or containers. The presence of copper or brass in the immediate vicinity can increase the chance of survival; copper corrosion products are poisonous to micro-organisms and could protect the finds from decay. This probably accounts for the survival of coloured compass cards, found inside their brass compass boxes despite centuries of burial in the seabed. In normal circumstances card does not survive.

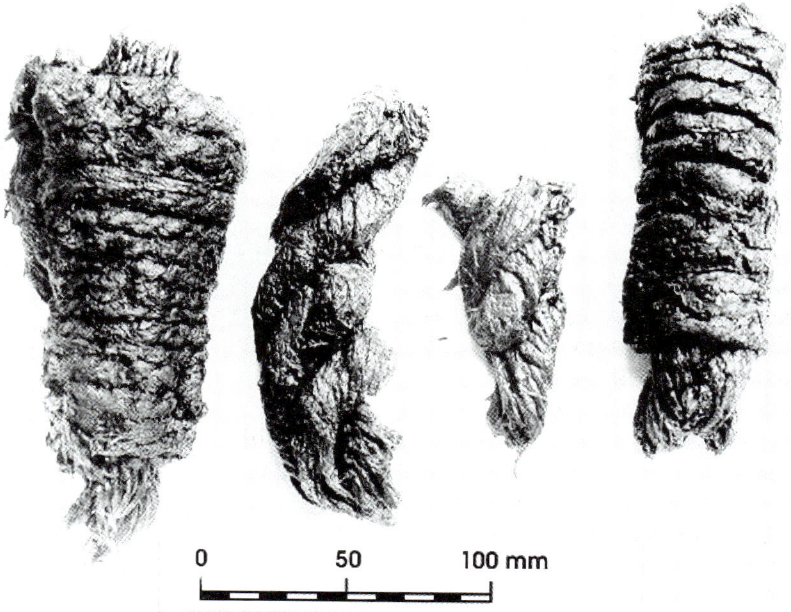

Fragments of rope from the wreck of the Santo Antonio de Tanna, *Mombasa. (W. Robinson)*

WARNING – URGENT ATTENTION REQUIRED

Have you found dyes or coloured decoration on basketry, clothing or matting? You may have discovered something very important that is highly unstable; take immediate action to protect it.

If you suspect that you might have found dyes, ink or pigmentation of any kind:

- keep the find in the dark
- do not clean the find – try to keep it covered in its burial deposit
- do not expose the find to biocides or to any other chemicals
- do not expose the find to light of any kind, and especially not photofloods
- investigate the possibility of having the find photographed in IR light
- consult a qualified conservator or archivist immediately

Remember that prompt action is essential.

Cordage and rope from shipwreck sites can be found in bulk. If buried near iron, they may be badly concreted, but such finds may also be little stronger than soft cheese.

Full conservation treatment

Treatment of textiles and documents requires the skills, expertise and dexterity of a qualified conservator. Fibres are easily damaged but textile and paper conservators are able to obtain a wealth of information from them: the type and origin of fibres; the twist and weave of threads; and even the most minute traces of inks, dyes or writing. In the wrong hands this evidence will be destroyed.

Sailcloth and rigging can present different problems owing to the vast quantities that may be survive on shipwreck sites. Excellent examples came from the Swedish warship, *Wasa,* where the ship had survived in the cold, oxygen-free waters of the Baltic. Other sites have produced material that is very soft and decayed, and often similar in consistency to the surrounding mud and silt. It will be unlikely that sailcloth can be unfolded, so do not attempt to do so, but a photographic or graphical record should be made. Close liaison with conservators, archaeologists and maritime specialists is essential whenever sailcloth and rigging are found.

A summary of first-aid treatments

Packaging for recovery from under the water

These items will be found in a highly degraded and very soft state, and extra care is needed to protect them. They should be handled as little as possible and placed in boxes or crates, packed or wrapped carefully under the water before being raised to the surface.

Initial storage on site

It is essential for these finds to be protected from the moment they are recovered. They should be kept in packing crates or boxes and not exposed to light. This may mean keeping transparent or translucent boxes covered. They will also need to be kept cool and transported to a conservation laboratory as soon as possible.

Cleaning

These finds are usually too fragile to be cleaned. A qualified conservator may gently use tweezers to remove loose debris from rope and rigging, but only from finds that are relatively sound. Concretions must not be removed by a non-specialist, as they will probably be much stronger than the find itself and may pull away some of the attached fibres. The concretion itself may also contain important evidence; an impression within the concretion crust. Such an impression on the wreck of the *Batavia*, Western Australia, was identified as that of a piece of lace, which had long since disintegrated (Pearson 1977).

Drying

On no account should these finds be dried as they will become brittle and will disintegrate.

Long-term storage

Small finds require prompt attention. Keep them in the wrappings they were given before being raised and take care to secure any loose fragments. They should receive minimum handling and must be kept at chilled temperatures (up to 4°C) and stored in darkened conditions. They should be taken to a qualified conservator as soon as possible.

Bulky items, like rope and sailcloth, that are too large to be refrigerated and that may soften in water will need different treatment. Generally they should receive minimal handling, but if sufficiently robust loose

SUMMARY

Sailcloth, rigging, textiles, weavings

These finds are highly unstable and very important. Handle them as little as possible.

- Carefully put them into boxes or crates under the water so that they will need minimum handling when raised.
- Immediately upon recovery keep them covered, cool and in darkened conditions.
- Finds should not be cleaned.
- Do not attempt to remove concretions as they may contain the impressions of decayed material.
- Store small finds in clean, fresh or tap water. Keep them chilled in darkened conditions and take them to a conservation laboratory as soon as possible.
- Larger finds should be sealed in boxes, lined crates or between layers of polythene. If conditions are not chilled change the water frequently to avoid biological growths.

detritus may be removed with gentle sprays of clean, chilled water. Finds must then be kept covered, packed and sealed, and stored in the dark at chilled temperatures. These are delicate materials and storage conditions must be thermostatically controlled and monitored daily. It is essential to consult a qualified conservator for further advice as soon as possible.

Solid foodstuffs (vegetable) and environmental material

Archaeological importance

The significance of these products is sometimes overlooked, although they are very important in the archaeological and environmental record. They can provide invaluable information about the trade links, social habits and living conditions of the time, as well as evidence of plants and animals that since may have become rare. Material of this kind should not be discarded; it could be very important.

Typical materials

Plant derivatives: seeds and grains; leafy material (eg tobacco or tea); vegetable and fruit remains (eg husks, stones and pips); spices.

Animal derivatives: insect and small animal remains, grubs and larvae; coprolites (fossilised droppings).

Typical finds

Food-store items; cargo items; substances used for packing (eg buckwheat); insect remains, (eg fleas and beetles), fly larvae; the bones of small fish or amphibians.

See Plate 16 (colour section page vii)

Composition and stability

Plant derivatives consist mainly of cellulose or lignin. They will therefore be highly unstable.

Animal derivatives are protein-based and have a better chance of survival. The hard wing cases of insects are particularly resistant to decay.

How these materials deteriorate

Anaerobic conditions are usually essential for the preservation of these materials. Remains may be found in sealed containers or in the silt deposits surrounding another object. They may also exist in the debris adhering to another find, or be found within the folds of a flexible material or garment. You must take great care not to wash them away. Many remains, like seeds or insect cases, will be very small, and specialist expertise and microscopic examination will be needed to identify them. Take care not to discard any material that may contain such remains. Do not attempt to clean finds or hunt for these remains yourself. Instead, consult an environmental specialist for further advice.

Full conservation treatment

A range of methods can be used to conserve these finds, although no treatment would ever begin until a specialist (environmental archaeologist) has provided advice on identification, interpretation and future research. They may be candidates for DNA screening, radiocarbon dating or examination by scanning electron microscope (SEM). Attempts have been made to use them to generate tissue cultures by taking samples; for example, with fruit stones found on the *Mary Rose*. With advances in plant science and genetic engineering, such experiments will undoubtedly one day meet with success. In the meantime, finds must be kept stable so that their potential for research is not destroyed.

A summary of first-aid treatments

Packaging for recovery from under the water

Finds and samples should be sealed in containers under the water and immobilised before being recovered. This will help to prevent cross-contamination.

Initial storage/cleaning

Once recovered they should receive minimal handling and be kept in their sealed containers, in cool and darkened conditions.

Do not attempt to clean or sort these finds, and watch out for similar remains adhering to fragments of other objects, particularly storage vessels, or surviving within the folds of clothing and footwear. If you find such evidence do not remove it but store the find, carefully packed so that these environmental remains do not become dislodged.

Drying

These finds and samples must be kept wet and never allowed to dry.

Long-term storage

Keep these finds immobilised, chilled and in darkened conditions. Store samples and loose finds in lidded boxes or sealed in polythene bags. Biocides must never be added. If you find material still packed inside a container or surviving within the folds of a garment, do not attempt to remove it.

SUMMARY

Solid foodstuffs and environmental remains

These finds and substances are very important as they can provide an information base for archaeologists, botanists, zoologists and ecologists.

- Keep finds and samples wet, chilled and in darkened conditions.
- If they are found within a container or adhering to other finds do not remove them.
- Biocides should not be used.

Liquid and semi-liquid (fatty/waxy) foodstuffs and preparations

Typical materials

Animal and vegetable fats, alcohol, beeswax.

Typical finds

These finds will most often be found within their original containers and should be kept there. Typical finds might include the contents of wine bottles or caskets of rum; ointments in small jars or caskets; tallow candles boxed in crates; wax seals on documents or sealing the corks of wine bottles; animal fats in wooden barrels.

Composition and stability

These substances provide rich nutrients for yeasts and bacteria and in general will only survive when such organisms are denied access. This can occur whenever storage vessels or containers survive sealed and intact with their contents undisturbed. Many examples have been recovered from shipwreck sites; for example, crates of bottles containing wine (oxidised to vinegar) and a barrel of animal fat (lard or butter) were recovered from the wreck of the *Amsterdam* in Hastings. Jars containing ointments were found on the *Mary Rose*, one of them retaining the embedded finger mark of the last Tudor who had used it.

Full conservation treatment

Owing to the diversity of these types of materials and the likelihood that they will be part of a composite object their conservation will be complex. Any treatment will be agreed between a conservator, archaeologist and finds specialist so that all conservation and research needs are met.

A summary of first-aid treatments

Cleaning

This must only be conducted under the supervision of a conservator. Loose silt and debris may be removed carefully from the outside of containers, but do not attempt to open any finds that are obviously sealed, as this may cause the contents to oxidise and decay.

Long-term storage

Containers and their contents should be kept immersed in water or sealed in polythene bags or wrappings and then stored at chilled temperatures in darkened conditions. It is most important to prevent corks in bottles from drying out, for in doing so they may shrink and allow oxygen into the bottle. Do not add chemicals of any kind and change the storage water if it becomes contaminated. Seek specialist advice as soon as possible.

SUMMARY

Liquids and semi-liquids, fats, oils, waxes

- Keep them in any containers in which they were found.
- Seek specialist advice from a qualified conservator.

Resinous and mineral substances of organic origin

Typical materials

Amber, jet, cannel coal, bitumen.

Typical finds

Amulets and ornaments, buttons and beads, jewellery, toys; tar and bitumen sealants or caulking materials.

Composition and stability

These substances derive from prehistoric plant or animal remains. They usually survive burial well and are generally stable but, unlike other mineral substances, will burn and may be harmed by organic solvents.

Amber is a plant resin that originally came from prehistoric conifers and was collected in ancient and historic times when washed up on the shore. It is usually yellow or gold in colour, and rare examples may have the perfectly preserved remains of extinct insects embedded within them. Amber needs special care as it is damaged by organic solvents (such as acetone or methylated spirits). Potentially harmful vapours may also leak from opened or poorly sealed solvent bottles, evaporate from discarded cleaning swabs or come from solvent-based adhesives, like those used to join pottery pieces. Take care to protect amber and never let it come into contact with organic solvents or vapours of any kind.

Jet and cannel coal are the transformed remains of prehistoric plants and were formed under high pressure and temperatures over geological periods of time. They are complex mixtures of hydrocarbons. Jet is a hard, compact black form of lignite (a form of coal) which can be carved and polished. In ancient times the main source of the jet industry was Whitby. Cannel coal is a bituminous coal, which, like jet, was valued in bygone times for its ability to be cut and polished into trinkets and jewellery.

Bitumen, like asphalt and tar, is a kind of mineralised pitch transformed from the decomposed remains of marine organisms, sand and silt. It has been used since ancient times.

Full conservation treatment

Following carefully monitored desalination in a conservation laboratory, these substances may be dried. They then need to be protected from excessive changes in temperature and relative humidity.

SUMMARY

Resinous and mineral substances of organic origin

These are usually found in good condition, but may start to laminate upon drying.

- Keep them wet and do not attempt to dry them, no matter how stable they may seem.

A summary of first-aid treatments

Desalination

Desalination processes should only be completed in a conservation laboratory with the proper facilities for monitoring and control. In certain circumstances, however, and on the advice of an archaeological conservator it may start at the first-aid site by placing the finds in changes of clean, fresh or tap water.

Drying

These finds must not be dried before desalination is complete.

Long-term storage

Keep the finds immersed in water, cold and in the dark. Monitor their condition regularly.

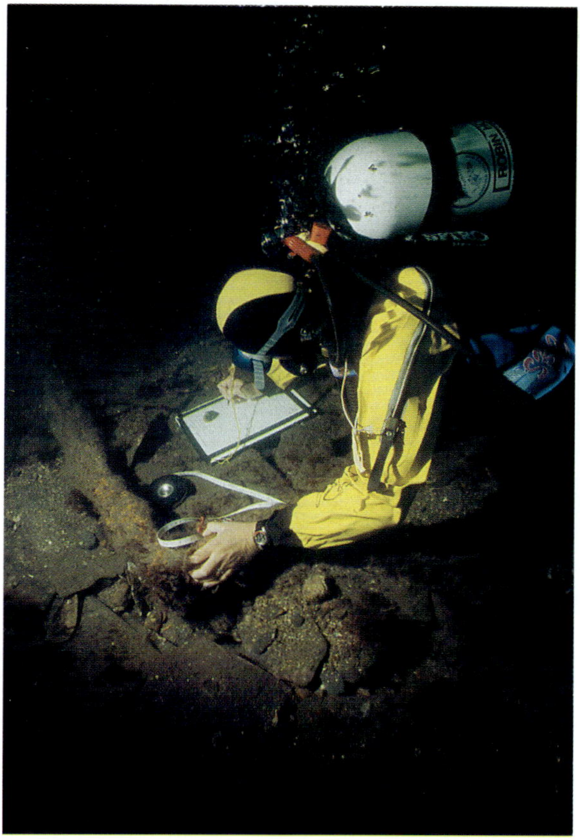

*1. Using archaeological methods to record the nineteenth century slate wreck (*John Preston*), Sound of Mull. (P. Robertson)*

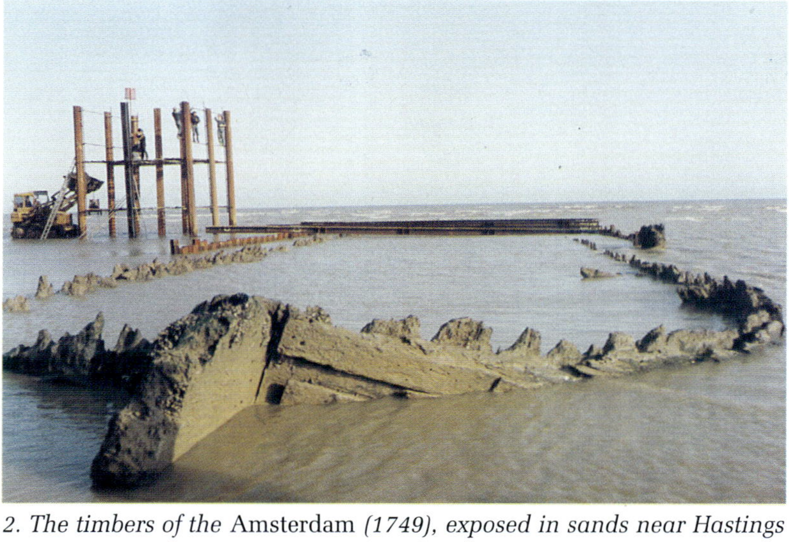

2. The timbers of the Amsterdam *(1749), exposed in sands near Hastings during low spring tides and showing erosion caused by the action of the sea. (W. Robinson)*

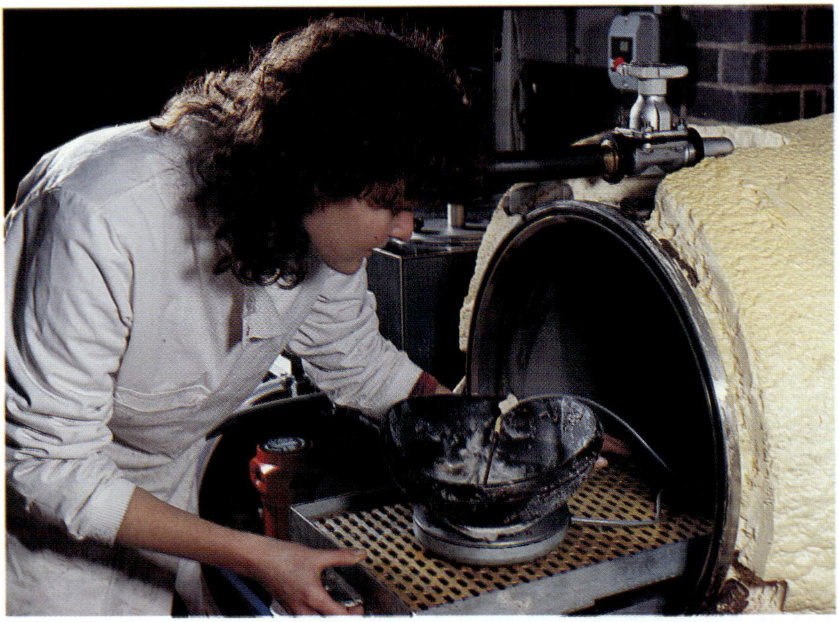

3. Wooden bowl being placed in freeze drier chamber. (Mary Rose Trust)

4. Wooden carve-fronted chest from the Mary Rose, *1545, treated and ready for display. (Mary Rose Trust)*

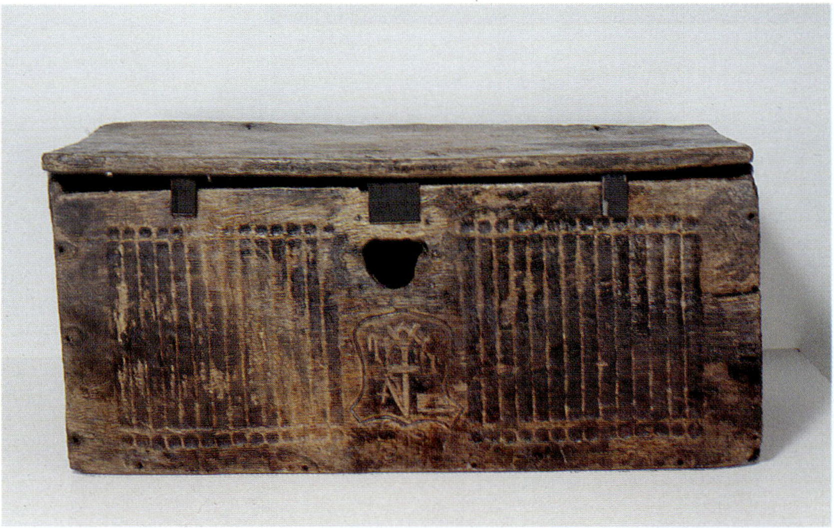

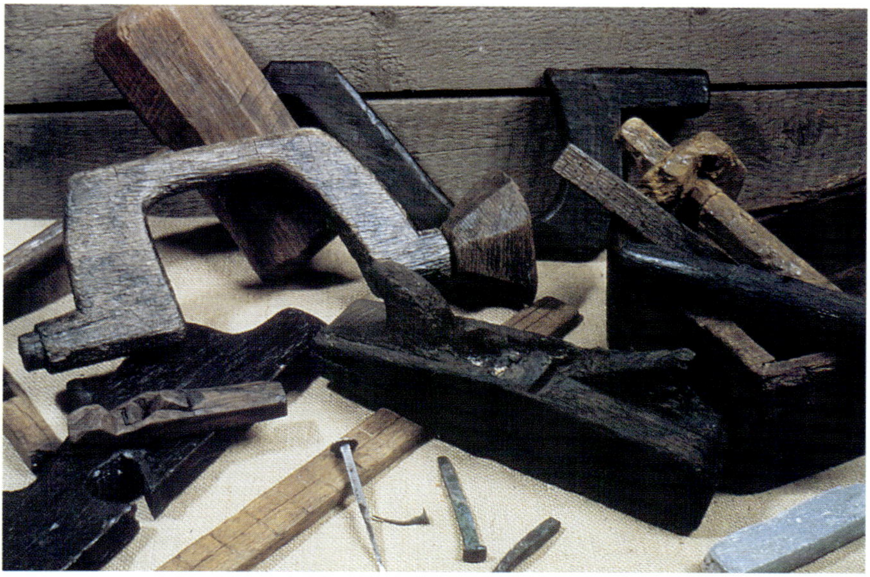

5. Wooden carpentry tools from a cabin on the main deck of the Mary Rose *including planes, braces, mortise gauge, whetstone and a ruler. In the foreground, a selection of nails. (Mary Rose Trust)*

6. Wooden blocks, deadeyes, line spacers, barrels and sheaves found on the Mary Rose. *(Mary Rose Trust)*

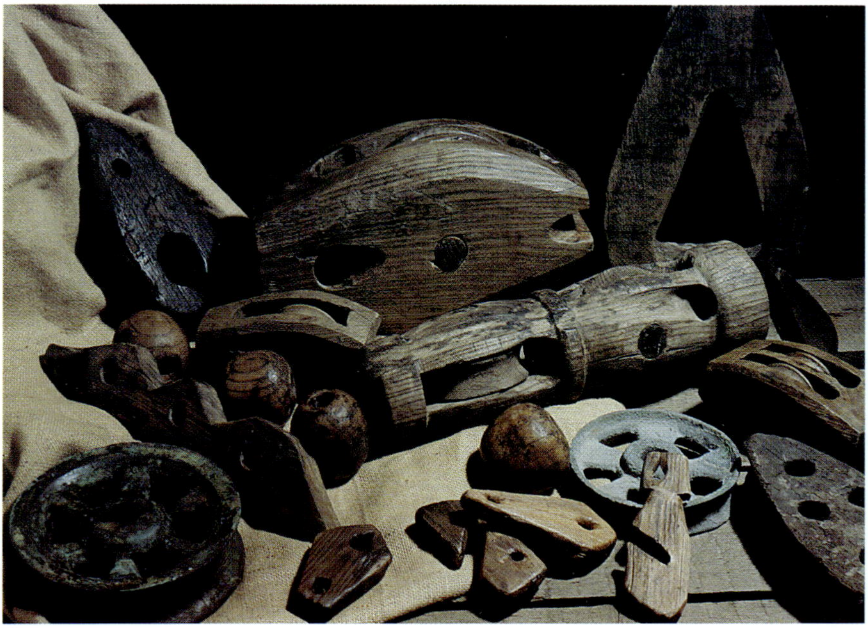

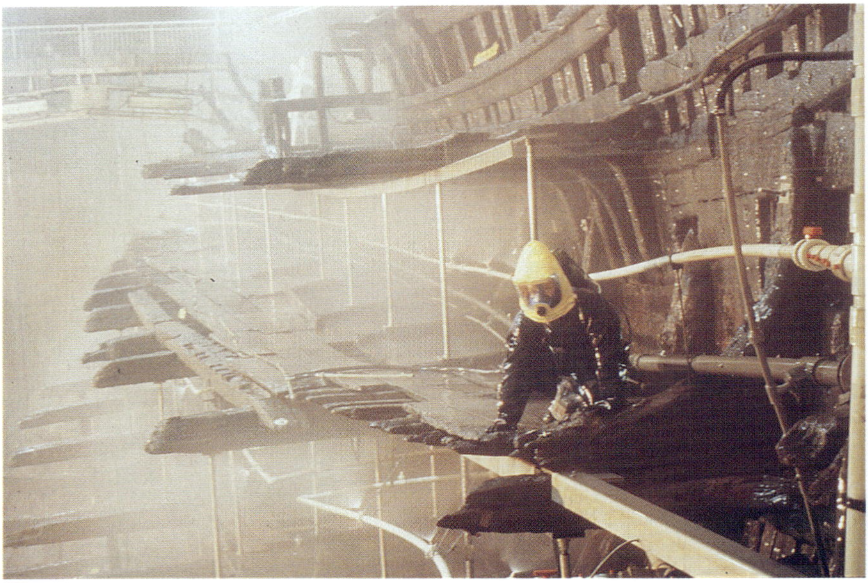

7. The Mary Rose *being sprayed with a fine mist of* PEG. *Here, a member of the conservation team inspects main deck timbers at the stern of the ship. (Mary Rose Trust)*

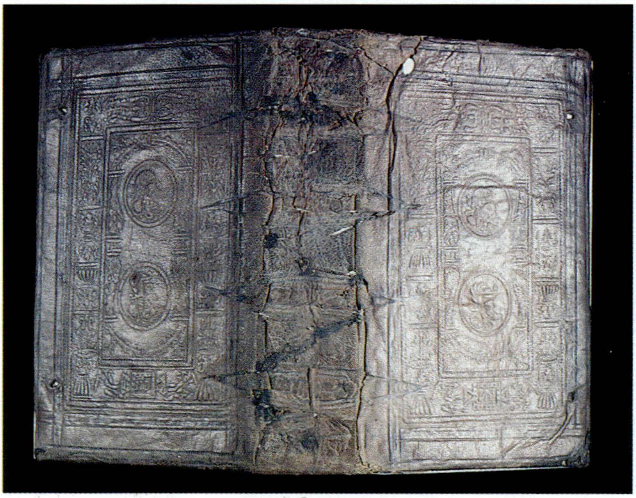

8. Leather book cover from the Mary Rose. *(Mary Rose Trust)*

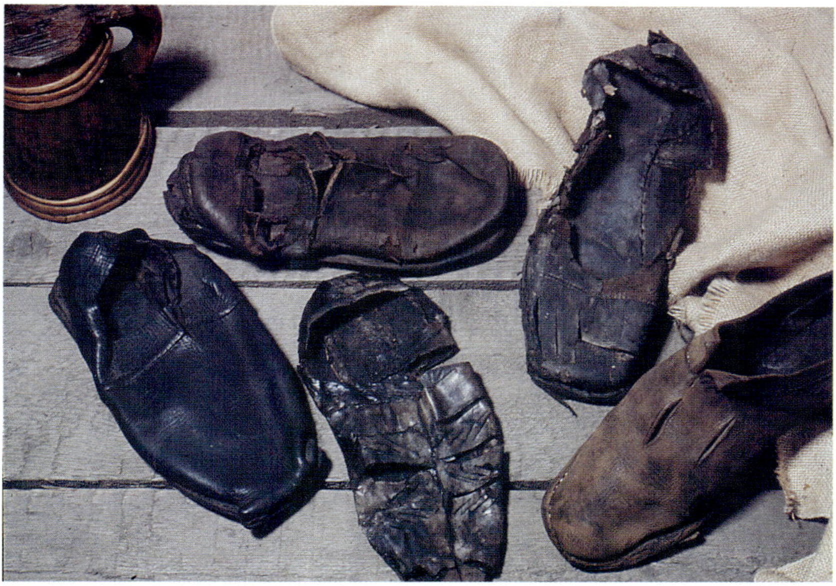

9. Some of the many leather shoes recovered from the Mary Rose. *(Mary Rose Trust)*

10. Some of the many personal items excavated from the Mary Rose, *including a leather pouch, wooden comb, seal, coins, pocket sundial, die, thimble-ring, clasp, whistle and rosary. (Mary Rose Trust)*

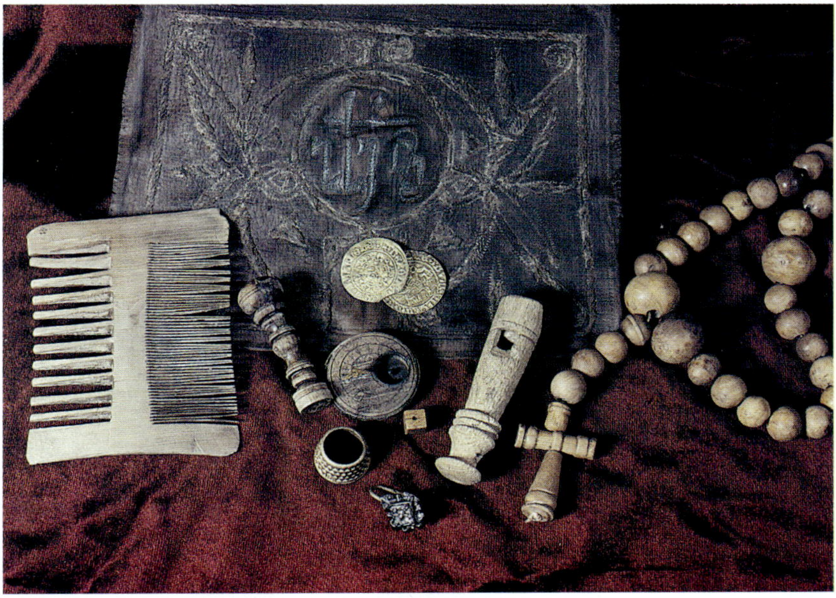

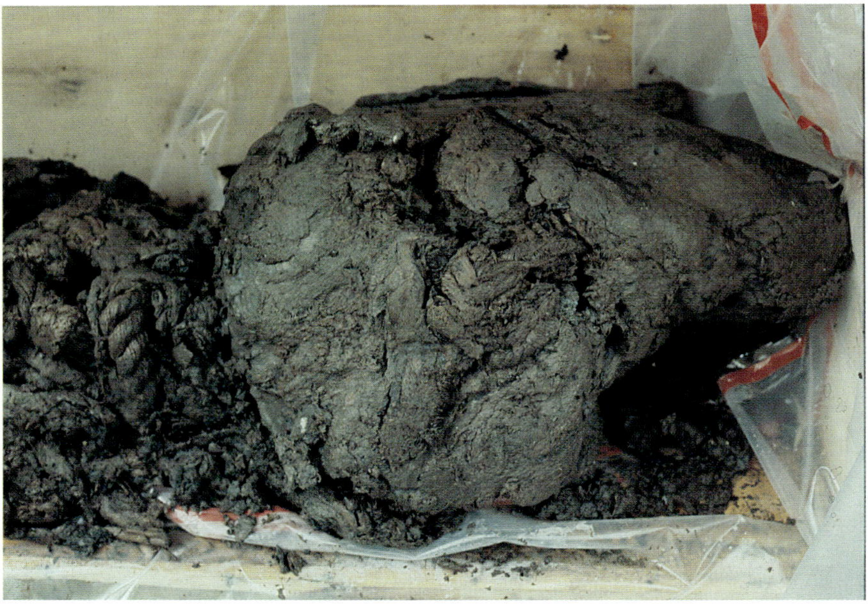

11. Remains of sailcloth and rigging from the wreck of the Santo Antonio de Tanna, *1667, Mombasa, Kenya. (W. Robinson)*

12. The medieval crannog site at Llangorse Lake, Wales, at which a piece of textile was found. (National Museum of Wales)

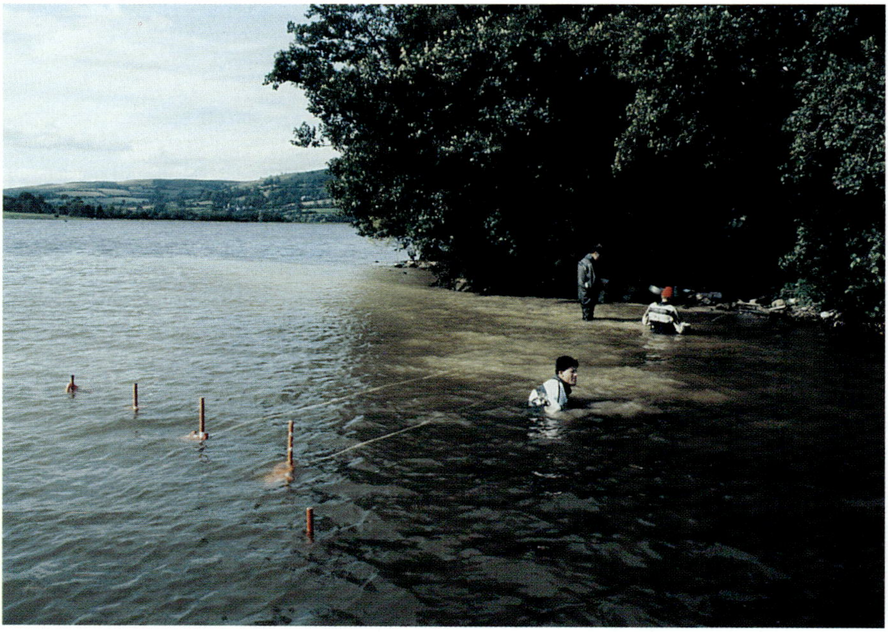

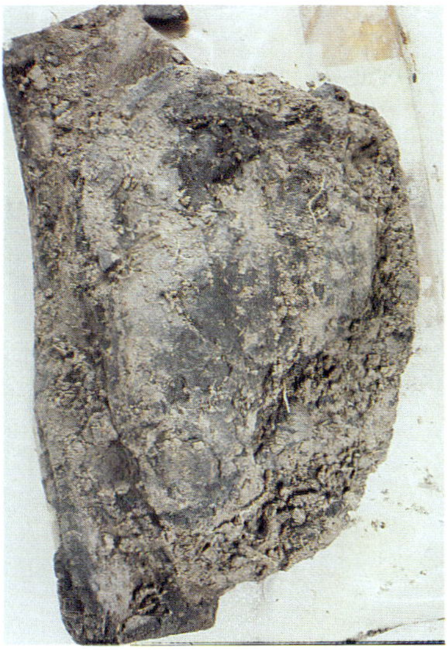

13. *Fragment of woollen textile found at Llangorse Crannog. (National Museum of Wales)*

14. *The same piece of textile following conservation. (National Museum of Wales)*

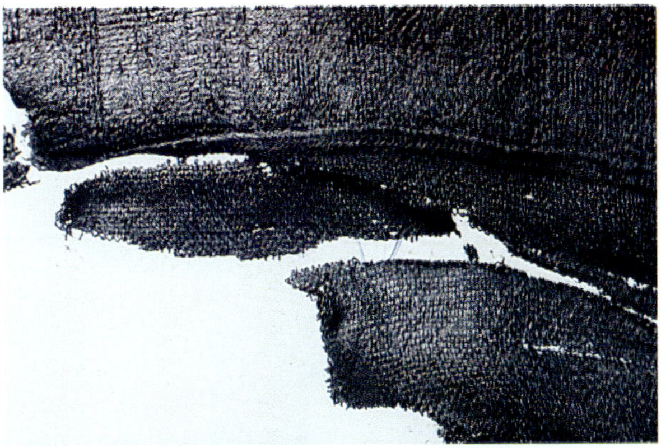

15. *Detail of the textile fragment from Llangorse Crannog. Notice the fine detail, still preserved since medieval times. (National Museum of Wales)*

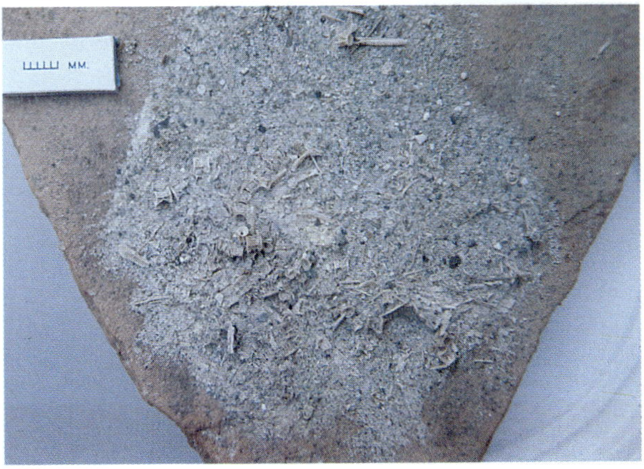

16. *The bones of small fish adhering to a fragment of Roman amphora. These formed part of the ship's cargo. (see Plate 21). (W. Robinson)*

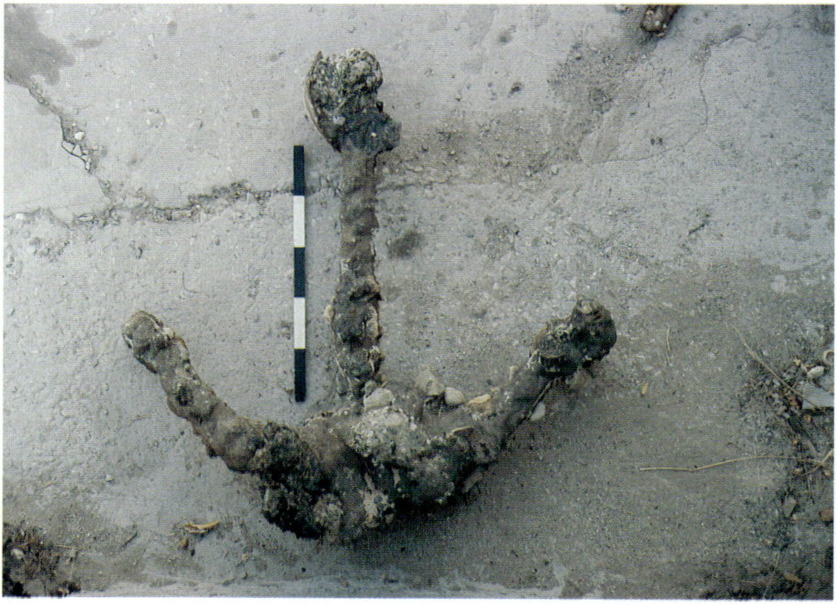

17. A Roman anchor from the Randello wreck, Sicily. The anchor was made from wrought iron and is heavily concreted. (W. Robinson)

18. Detail of the wrought iron anchor concretion from Randello. Inside the concretion the iron had completely gone, leaving a hollow cavity which could be used as a mould. Next to the hollow fragment is a rubber cast taken from the concretion mould showing the end of the original anchor shaft. (W. Robinson)

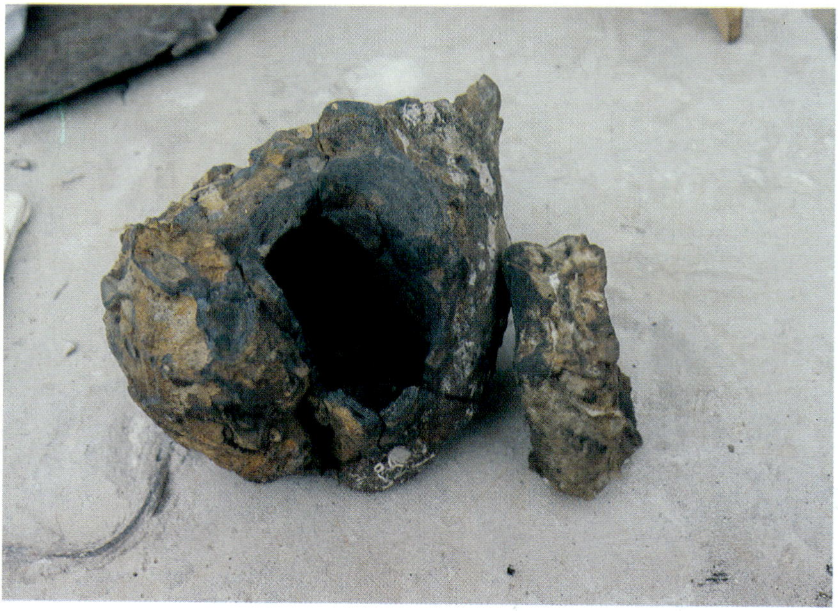

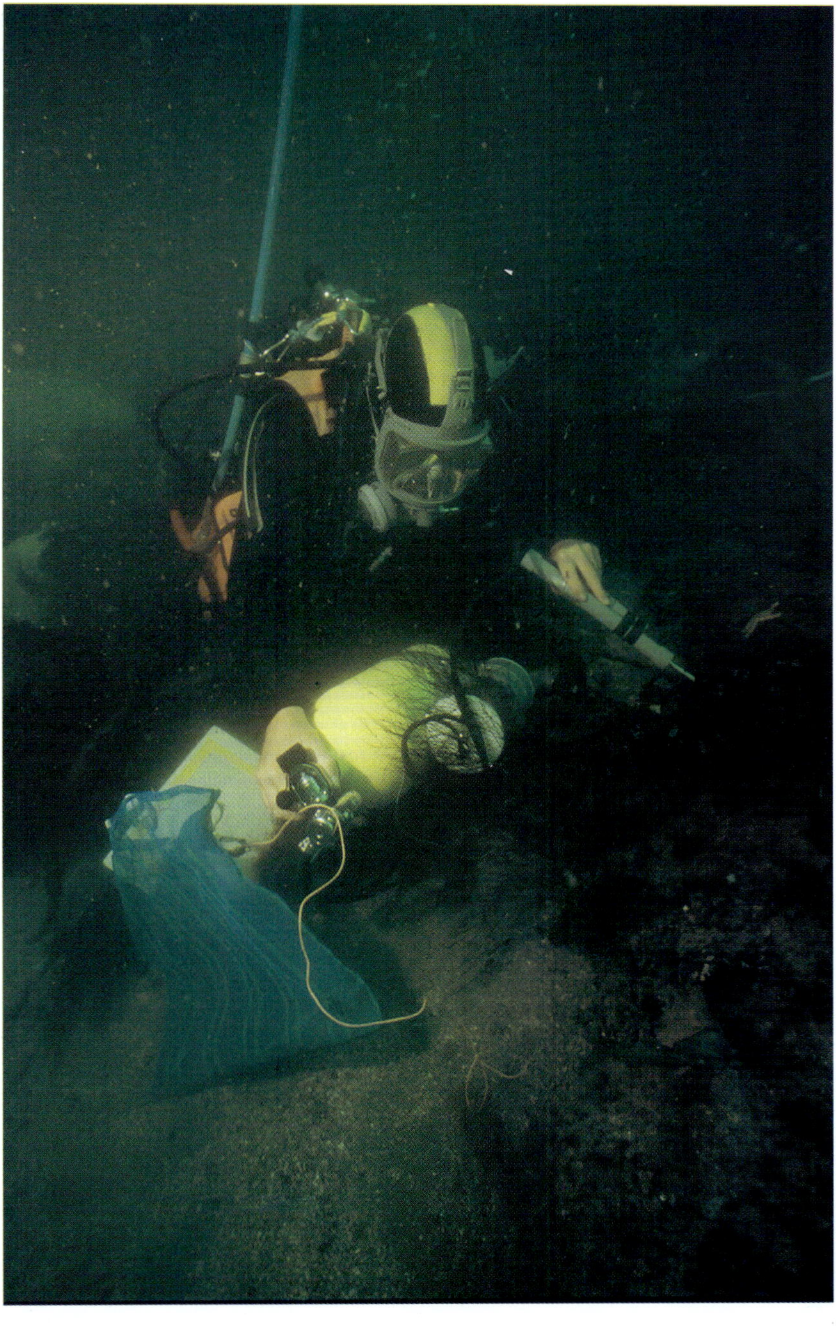

19. Dr Dave Gregory taking underwater corrosion readings from a cannon from the Swan, *at Duart Point. (P. Robertson)*

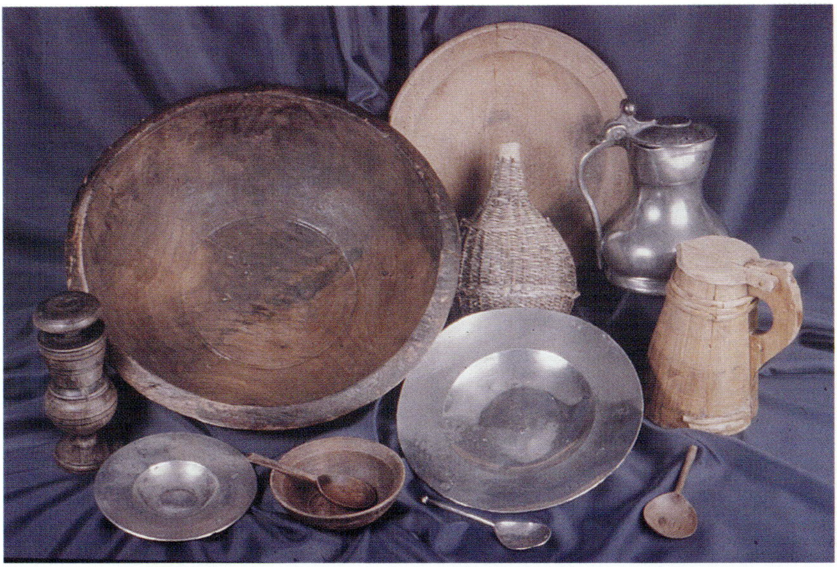

20. A group of domestic items from the Mary Rose, *including a pewter flagon, spoon and plates. (Mary Rose Trust)*

21. Roman amphorae found buried in sand at the wreck at Randello, Sicily. The site was covered by little more than 3 metres of water, yet the amphorae still held remains of their original contents – carefully packed sardine-like fish. (See Plate 16 for a close-up photograph of some of the fish-bones). Each amphora stands about 1.5 metres high. (W. Robinson)

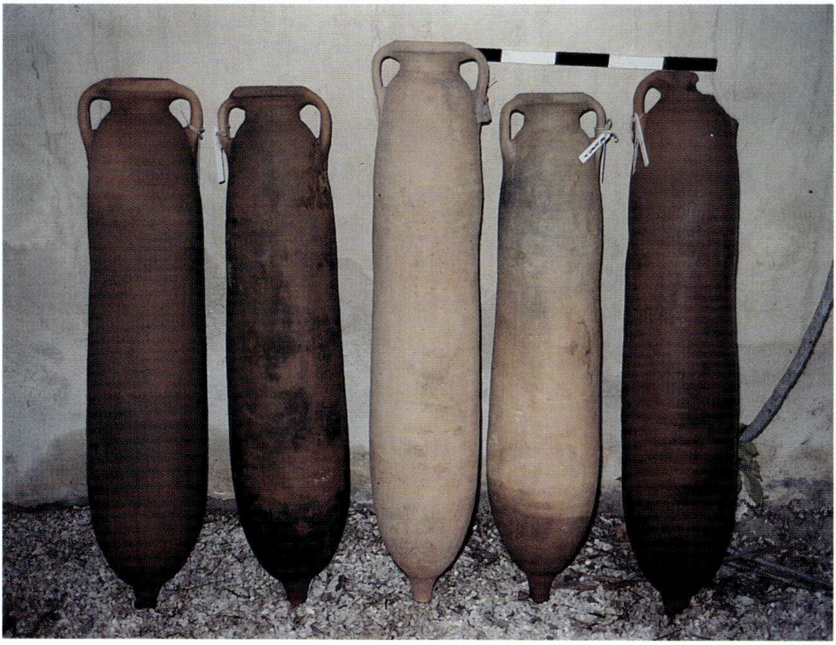

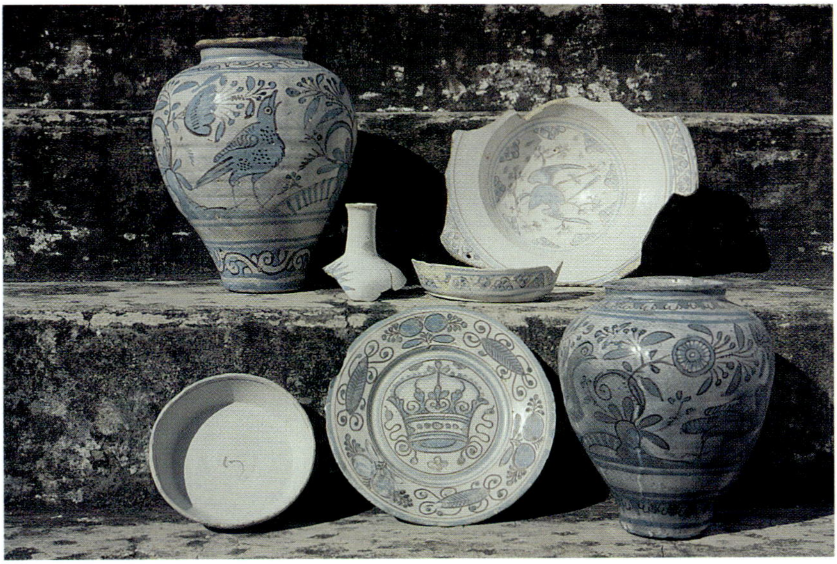

*22. Tin-glazed ceramics from the 17th century wreck at Mombasa (*Santo Antonio de Tanna, *1667). On one of the jars the tin-glaze has become blackened. (W. Robinson)*

23. A wicker-bound glass flask from the Mary Rose. *(Mary Rose Trust)*

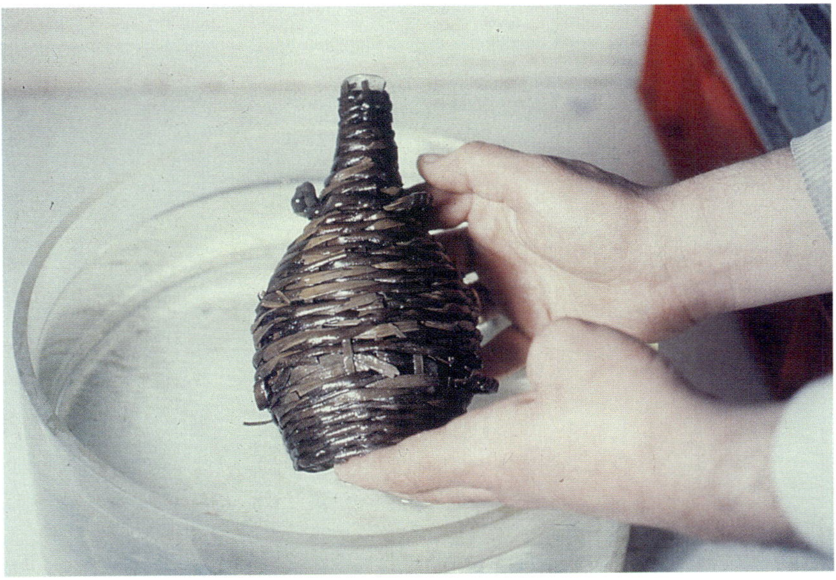

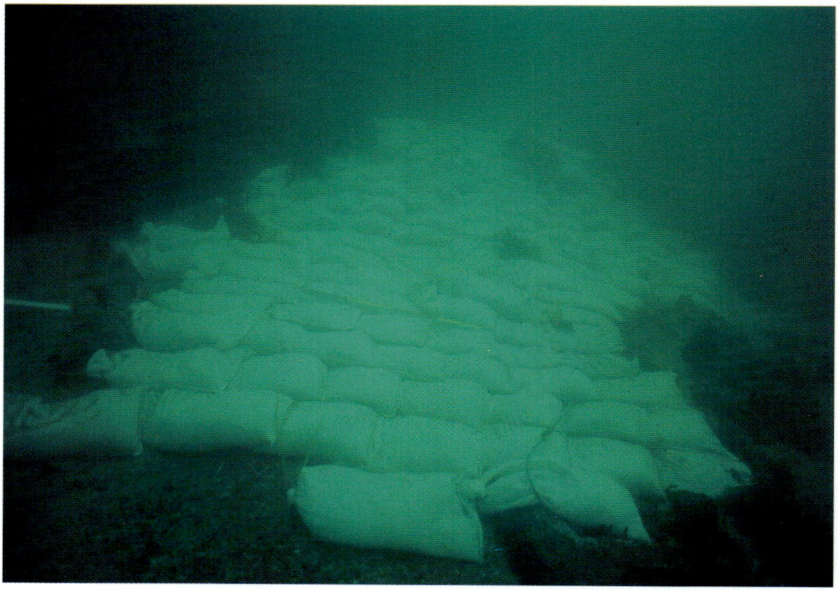

24. A single skin of shingle-filled sandbags in place over an eroding organic deposit on the Duart Point wreck. (C. Martin)

25. A seventeenth century ship's compass being recorded shortly before being raised from the Swan *at Duart Point. (P. Robertson)*

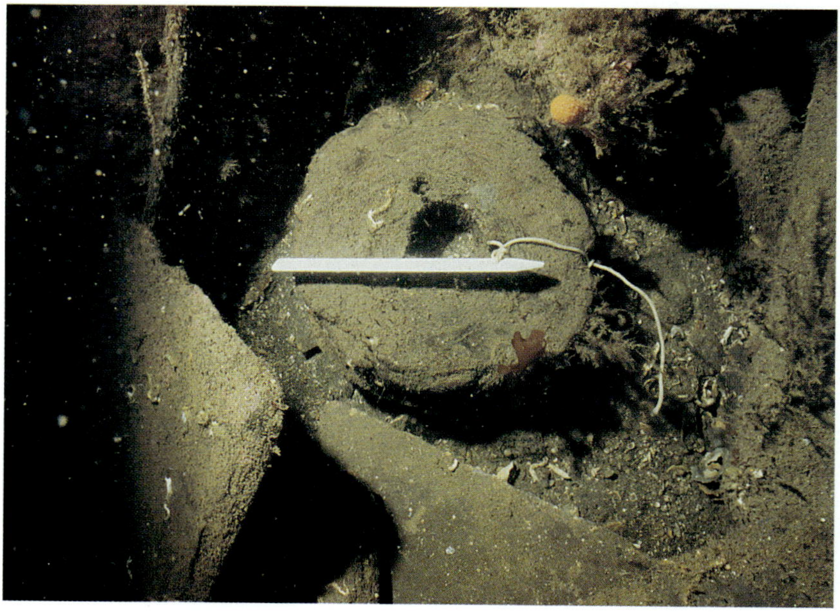

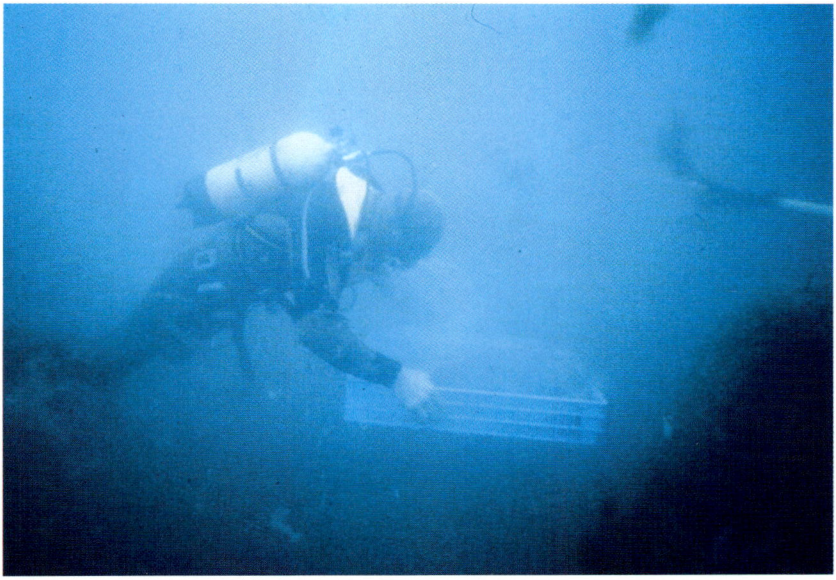

26. Moving objects from the Mary Rose *underwater. (Mary Rose Trust)*

27. Clearing trenches in preparation for raising the medieval boat at Magor Pill, Gwent. (The National Museum of Wales)

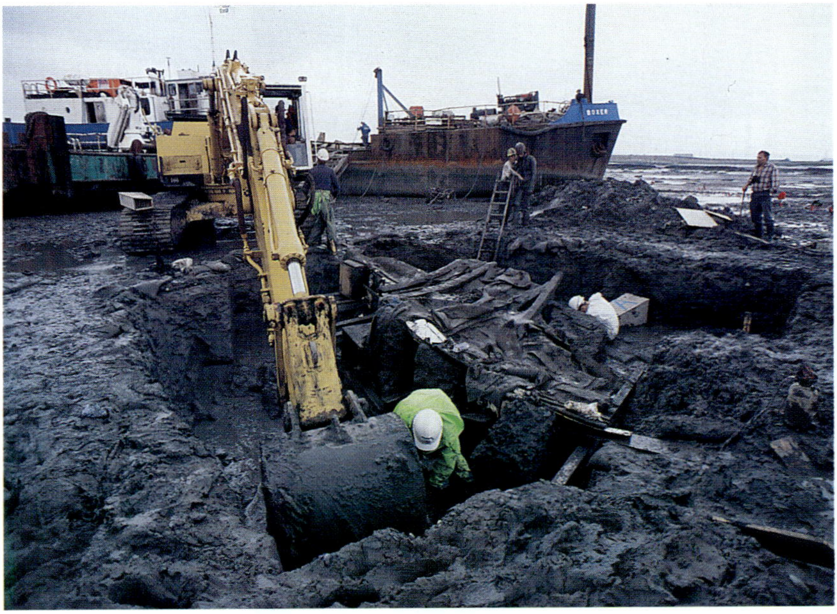

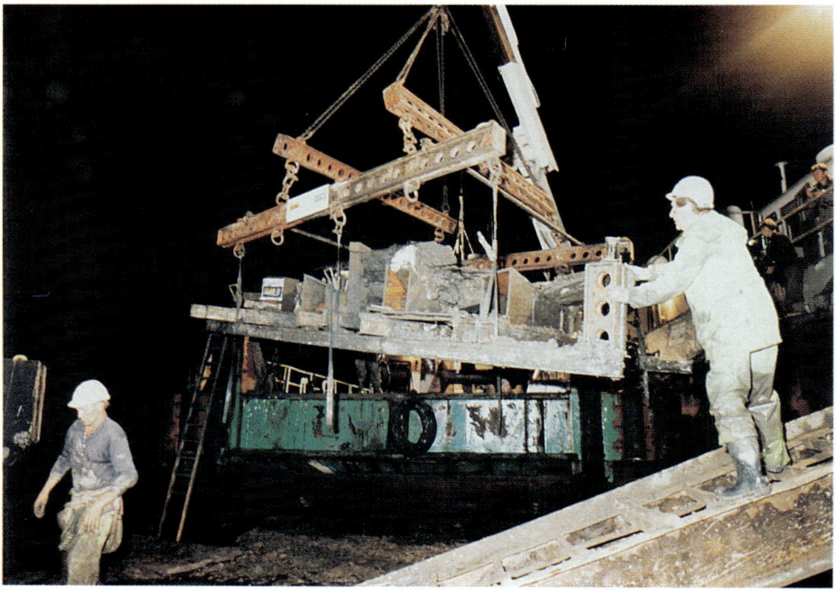

28. Lifting the Magor Pill boat. (The National Museum of Wales)

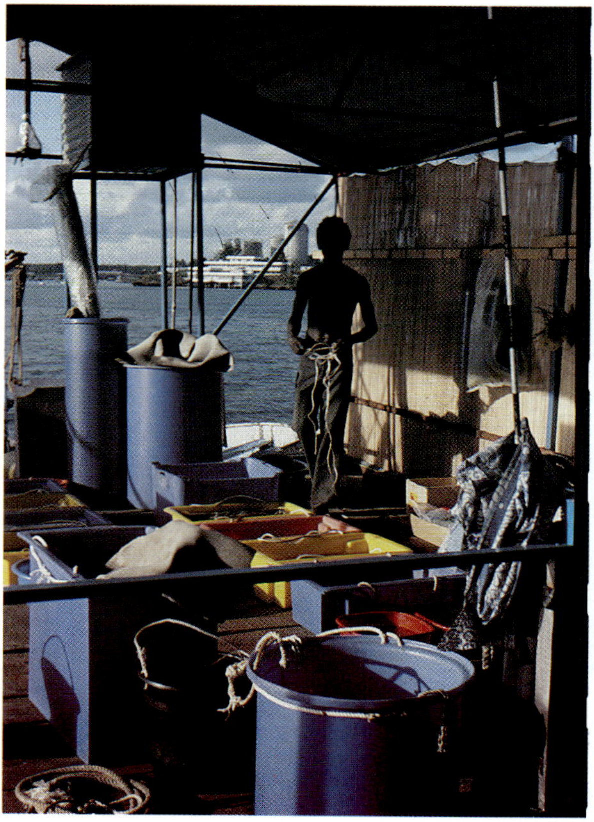

29. Storage containers on board the recovery vessel at Mombasa, in preparation for finds from the wreck of the Santo Antonio De Tanna, *1667. (W. Robinson)*

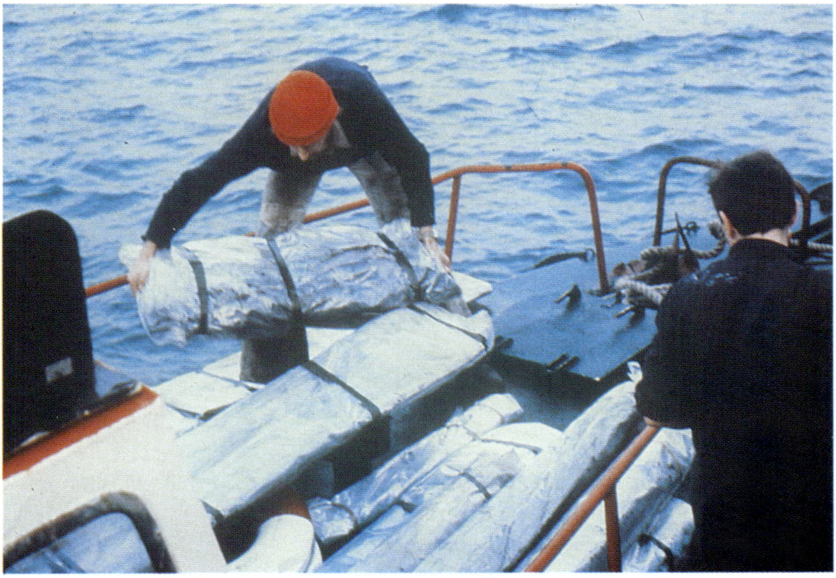

30. Transportation of objects from the Mary Rose *ashore. (Mary Rose Trust)*

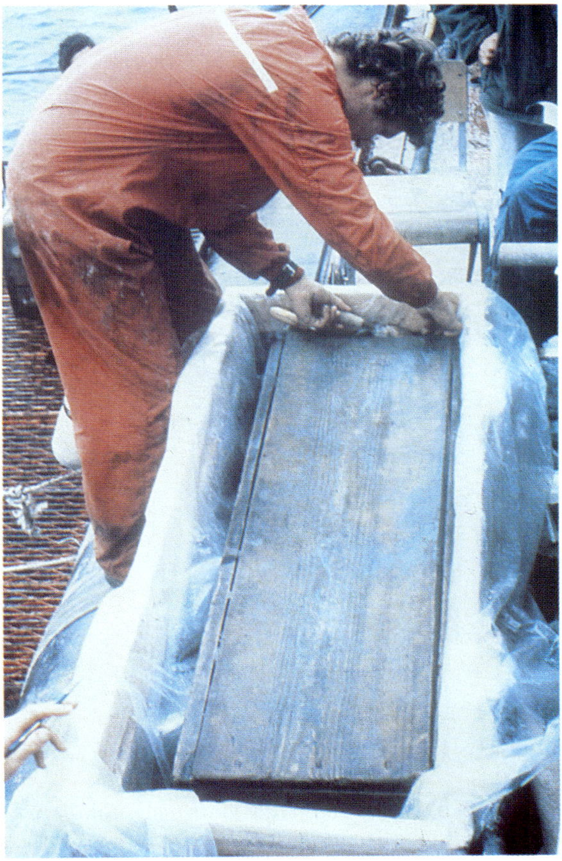

31. Excavation of a chest from the Mary Rose. *(Mary Rose Trust)*

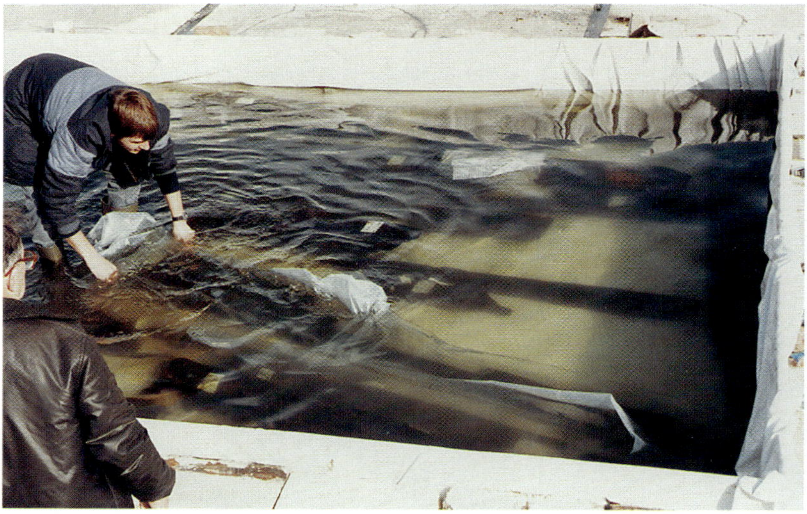

32. Temporary storage of timbers from the Amsterdam *(1749) in a former paddling pool at Bexhill-on-sea. (W. Robinson)*

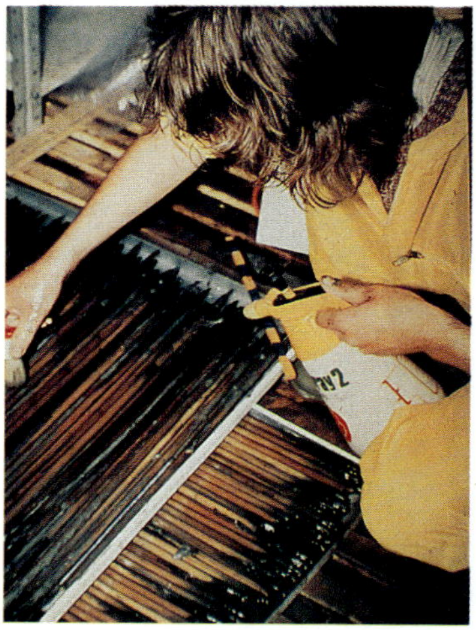

33. A conservator carefully cleaning arrows from the Mary Rose. *(The Mary Rose Trust)*

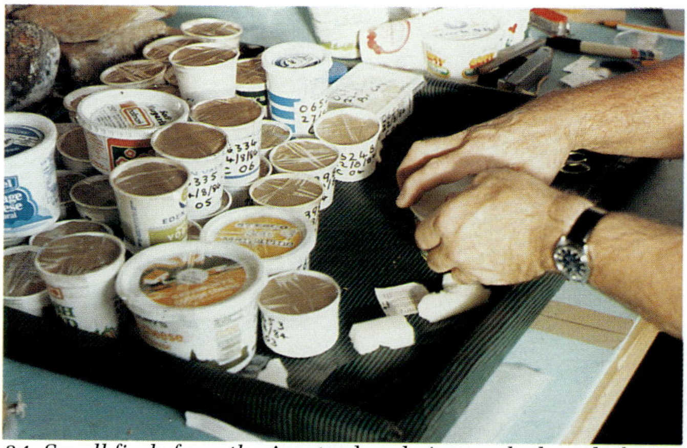

34. Small finds from the Amsterdam *being packed ready for transportation in a refrigerated container and conservation in Holland. (W. Robinson)*

5 Metals

Survival

It is likely that a wide range of metals or alloys will be found at underwater sites. They may take the form of the pure metal, (such as pig iron, copper, lead, silver or gold) or alloys (such as wrought or cast iron, bronze, brass, gun metal, solder, pewter, sterling silver and electrum).

Typical finds are scrap metal, ingots or ballast, coinage and worked or cast artefacts of various types. Metal inlays, overlays, platings or other surface coating were often used to decorate other objects. In ancient times, for example, some Roman coins were given a surface coating of tin or silver to make them appear more valuable. These surface coatings will probably have become obscured, especially if they have become embedded within the corrosion products of an underlying base metal. They may even have become transformed into corrosion products themselves. For this reason, adherent corrosion products should never be removed from metal objects. X-ray examination may be necessary to reveal them.

The survival and condition of any particular metal or coating will depend upon a range of factors including:

- the nature of the metal or the components of the alloy
- features of the manufacturing process and the use to which the object was put
- the nature of the burial environment (oxygen content, acidity/alkalinity, quantity and nature of dissolved salts, chemical composition, particle size, amount and type of bacteria)
- direct contact with another metal or the presence of other metals or concretions in the vicinity.

Identification

Individual metals can sometimes be recognised by the characteristic colour of their surface or corrosion products. A rough guide to identification is given below.

Guide to the identification of metals by the nature of their corrosion products.

Metal	Guide to corrosion products
Copper and copper alloys (including brass and bronze)	Dark red and purple corrosion layers. Green/yellow compounds. Black deposits.
Iron	Black corrosion products, which are sometimes magnetic. Rust-coloured layers. Red and yellow compounds. Soft, green innermost corrosion layers. (Iron corrosion products may be found on the surface of all other metals and substances. However, a magnet will detect the presence of metallic iron.) When iron is found in rich organic contexts (high in phosphate) it may be covered by a thin white layer, which turns deep blue upon exposure to light.
Lead	Crystalline corrosion products (grey or white). White or buff surface deposits in very thin layers.
Pewter (tin/lead alloy)	Grey surface, often with wart-like eruptions. The metal may be soft and metallic or friable and crystalline.
Silver	White layers, perhaps wax-like, which turn purple on exposure to light. Black, amorphous deposits. Sometimes crystalline and friable metallic structures.

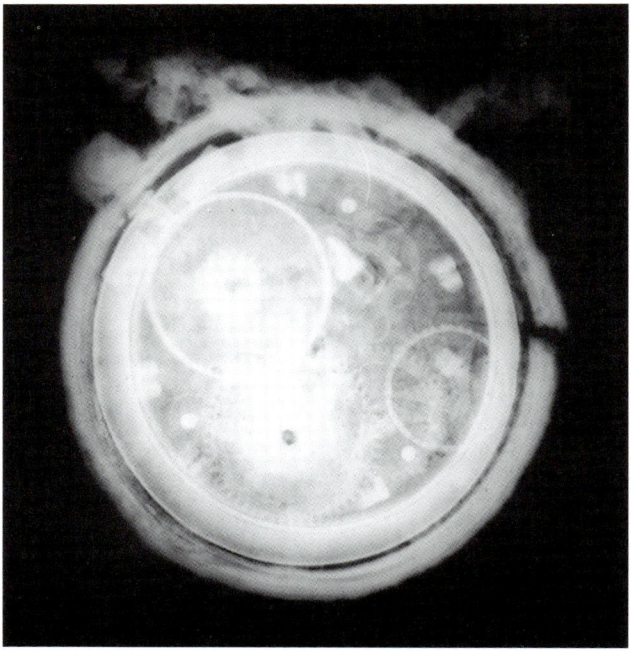

An X-ray of a pocket watch from the Duart Point wreck (the Swan, 1653), Scotland, showing the intricate detail of wheels and cogs inside. (National Museums of Scotland)

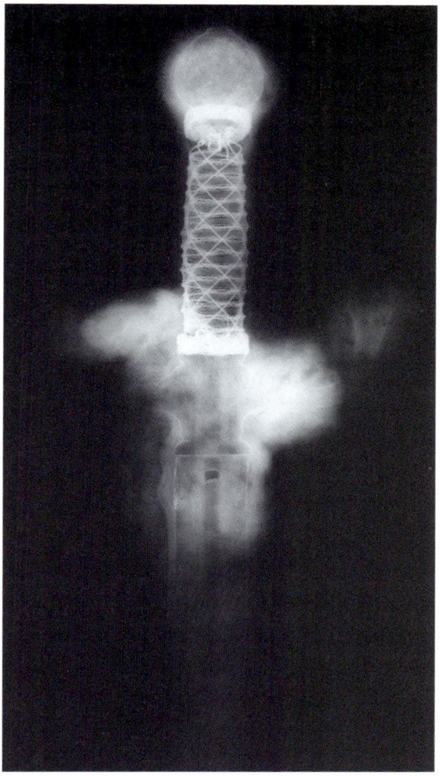

The fine details of the hilt and blade of a rapier from the Swan, *Duart Point, have been revealed in this* X*-ray. (National Museums of Scotland)*

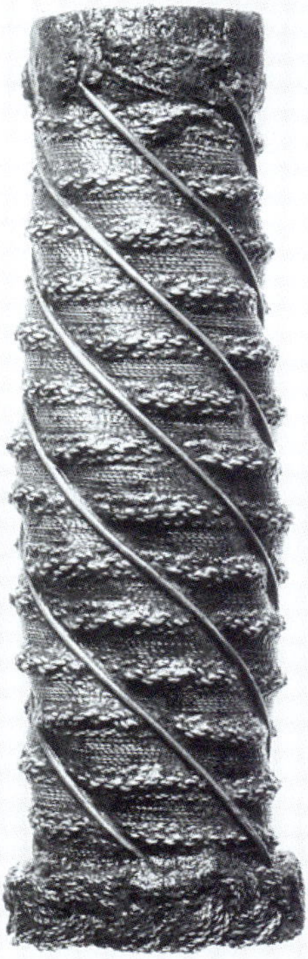

The Duart Point sword hilt after removal from concretion. This composite object incorporated the ferrous remains of the tang, a wooden core, and gold and silver decorative windings. (C. Martin)

Stability

Even though some metals survive burial underwater over long periods, most become highly unstable when they are exposed to new burial or water conditions or to the atmosphere. The metal at greatest risk is iron (in all its forms). Corrosion rates have been monitored and are found to increase one hundred-fold during excavation and shortly afterwards (MacLeod 1987, 51). Bubbles may be seen coming from the surface of the metal, showing that corrosion is active, and in some cases the metal starts to heat up alarmingly. Eventually the find cracks and starts to disintegrate.

In wet and damp conditions metals corrode by electrochemical means, a process that involves a flow of electrons. When two metals come together in an electrolyte (water and dissolved salts), one of them usually becomes an anode, and corrodes in preference to the other

FIRST-AID ESSENTIALS

Metals and alloys

Finds must be protected from:

- the possibility of renewed attack, either during excavation or following recovery.
- stresses and strains during lifting, recovery and transportation.
- the removal of corrosion products and any form of surface cleaning.
- corrosion during storage.

Store different metals separately and only add a corrosion inhibitor upon conservation advice.

metal, the cathode. Metal finds, therefore should be sorted and each stored separately.

Concretions

Concretions are a characteristic feature of marine sites whenever iron is present. Corrosion products from iron combine with seawater to form heavy and dense concretions.

Full conservation treatment

Current methods of treating large metal objects from marine environments are based on electrolytic reduction (although for land-based finds, with lower chloride contamination, this method was discontinued years ago). During this process the find is wired to a battery or DC source of electricity to become the cathode. A suitable anode (usually platinum) is connected to the other terminal, and the cell is completed by placing the find and anode into an electrolyte. When a small current is applied, chloride ions – the primary agents of corrosion – are attracted from the find to the anode. If carried out correctly and thoroughly, electrolytic reduction can have very good rates of success, although large objects may take several years to treat. If carried out incorrectly, however, the process may result in destruction of the artefact, with its shape and surface destroyed beyond recognition and any alloy components leached away. Alternative methods involve treatment with corrosion inhibitors, but these are lengthy and expensive processes.

Following conservation, metals still need protecting from moisture in the atmosphere or condensation. They must be stored or displayed in controlled, stable conditions where relative humidity is very low (less than 35%; for ironwork, less than 15%).

Ferrous metals (cast iron, wrought iron, steel, concretions)

Typical materials

Wrought iron, cast iron, mild steel.

Typical finds

Pig iron ballast; hull cladding; tools, equipment and machinery parts; blades, weaponry, cannon, guns and armour; shot and cannon balls, anchors; barrel hoops, horse shoes, nails; locks and keys.

Composition

Wrought iron, used in the west since the Iron Age, is made by hammering at red heat the malleable metal product of the smelting process. Wrought iron contains little carbon, and the hammering elongates any remaining slag inclusions (silicates and the metal oxides) into 'stringers'. During corrosion, preferential attack of the iron around the stringers gives the metal a fibrous appearance. Ancient repairs were made by 'hammer welding', and these too may be revealed as corrosion progresses.

Cast iron (pig iron), the primary product of the blast furnace, became generally available in Europe from 1389. It contains a high amount of carbon (between 2% and 4%) which enhances its casting qualities but increase its brittleness. Some of the carbon in 'grey' cast iron is present as graphite. Corrosion of the iron can leave a fragile graphite 'skeleton'; a process known as graphitisation.

Steel is also manufactured from pig iron and contains between about 0.1% and 1.9% carbon. During the manufacturing process impurities are removed and other elements, such as manganese, titanium, chromium or vanadium, are added to improve its strength. Carbon steel, with varying amounts of carbon and up to 1.65% manganese with small amounts of silicon and copper is now used for ships hulls.

Ferrous metals usually corrode to form 'concretions'; conglomerates of corrosion products and debris from the burial environment. In non-marine environments these may form as spongy masses, thin rusty crusts or much harder layers. Concretions may be found covering finds of any type, or appear in apparent isolation, mobile corrosion products having precipitated from a source elsewhere. On marine sites, concretions are characteristically hard and dense and extricating them may be very difficult. They may contain a wealth of material or archaeological evidence, some of a very fragile nature. Some concretions have been found to retain impressions of material that perished long ago – examples from the *Batavia*, in Australia, had formed impressions of delicate lace that itself had not survived. They may also encapsulate a host of other finds and preserve them from destruction: it is not unusual to discover conglomerations of objects and marine debris concreted into one amorphous mass. Other concretions form on iron itself. Those on cast iron usually retain the original find preserved inside, but others, especially from wrought iron or mild steel may be hollow. These can, none the less, be of archaeological value: the hollow concretion may have formed a perfect mould of the original object. Flexible casting materials, such as silicone rubber and sometimes rubber latex can be applied to take a cast. X-ray examination can detect the contents of concretions and should be routinely carried out.

Stability

All forms of iron are highly unstable and the metal can corrode in both oxygen-rich and oxygen deficient conditions. The rate of iron corrosion can be particularly fast when other metals are present, when burial conditions change or when the metal is exposed to atmospheric conditions.

Particularly unfortunate examples of unstable iron are the sunken hull remains of nineteenth or early twentieth century vessels. Experience has taught that, when first recovered, they often appear to be in an excellent state, and their salvors may marvel at how well they have been preserved. But corrosion soon sets in, fuelled by oxygen in the atmosphere and enhanced by an array of other types of metal fittings, which also formed parts of these hulls. The structures then begin to disintegrate alarmingly and this cannot be stopped. In such circumstances it might have been better not to raise them at all.

How iron corrodes

Iron can be attacked in all kinds of damp or waterlogged conditions, with and without oxygen. The metal is highly reactive and corrodes by 'rusting' and by electrochemical means. Sea-water, with a plentiful supply of dissolved salts to make it electrically conductive, is an ideal electrolyte, but minute traces of moisture on the surface of iron, or held within its crystalline structure will also suffice.

As well as a potential difference (eH) arising between two dissimilar metals, creating an anode and a cathode, the same effect can arise at local points on or within a single metal. The presence of impurities or alloying materials within a metal may cause such an eH gradient, or it may be that one part of the metal is slightly different from another part. Exposed/unexposed, worked/unworked, and scratched/undamaged areas may all trigger electrochemical corrosion: think of the corrosion on car bodywork.

In marine conditions, corrosion processes for wrought and cast iron have different end results. Wrought iron characteristically forms a dense concretion crust which builds up on the surface of the metal. During this process, corrosion products migrate away from the object and re-deposit on the surface of the concretion. In extreme cases the original find may disappear completely, leaving only a black 'sludge'. However, the shape of the find is often retained within the concretion shell. This can be revealed by x-ray examination, and casting materials can be used to make a replica of the original. This does occur in non-marine conditions too, but at a much slower rate.

See Plates 17 and 18 (colour section, p. viii)

Cast iron is not known to form hollow concretions. Instead the original find may still be within the concretion crust, most likely in a graphitised state. This is because cast iron is composed of a network of carbon-rich components (graphite or cementite) intermingled with structures of the more pure metal (pearlite). Minute electrochemical cells form between these components and corrosion products form within, rather than away from, the object. As a result the shape of the find is preserved, although in a very fragile state.

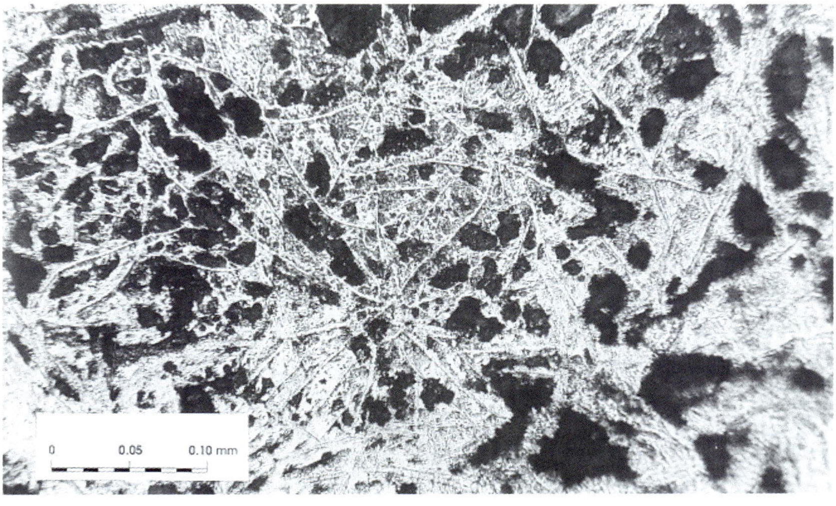

A micro-photograph of a fragment of cast iron cannon ball. The string-like features are flakes of graphite, seen end-on and surrounded by corrosion products. This is typical of the 'graphitisation' of cast iron. (W. Robinson)

On rare occasions, in such conditions as stagnant waters, wells or waterlogged deposits where phosphate levels are high, perhaps as a result of decaying bones, iron seems to defy normal processes of corrosion. Instead a protective layer of iron phosphate forms (vivianite), which is white at first but changes to a deep blue on exposure to light. This layer effectively seals the metal and serves to restrict the progression of corrosion reactions. The coating may be damaged by damp, oxygen-rich conditions and special care must be taken whenever it is found.

RECOVERING IRON? THINK AGAIN!

Iron is difficult to conserve and is best left *in situ*.

Full conservation treatment

The conservation of iron is extremely problematic and even after decades of research and experimentation there is no easy answer. The aim of treatment is to remove all traces of the chloride ions that initiate or catalyse corrosion, remove all moisture by drying, and then protect the remaining iron from further attack. A range of conservation treatments have been devised over the years, suitable for use in different situations. One method that used to be popular was to roast the iron in a hydrogen reduction furnace. This produced apparently good results, but was archaeologically unsound owing to the loss of surface detail of the metal, and, more importantly, because the process destroyed important scientific information held within the metallographic structure. The method is no longer widely used or recommended.

One promising method for treating marine iron, which has the additional benefit of not requiring finds to be raised, is the use of sacrificial anodes. Sacrificial anodes have been used to protect floating steel hulls and underground pipes for some time, and Australian conservators have been adapting this method for iron that is still on the seabed (Macleod 1987, 1995). These conservators, along with others, had observed that the corrosion of iron proceeded at alarming rates as the environment was disturbed during excavation. They experimented with *in situ* stabilisation, monitoring the method by taking corrosion readings underwater, and are now pioneering *in situ* stabilisation methods. Once again electrochemical corrosion is involved, but this time it is controlled so that the iron benefits and other metals are sacrificed: some metals are even more electrochemically reactive than iron and will corrode in preference. Zinc is such a metal, and has been used in the past by engineers to afford 'anodic protection' to buried pipes. Conservators have adapted the method by attaching strips or scrap items of zinc next to marine iron that is still submerged. The zinc becomes the anode, so corrosion reactions take place on the zinc. Eventually the zinc will corrode completely (the 'sacrificial' anode) and have to be replaced, but until then corrosion reactions on the iron effectively stop forming. Results are encouraging, and even suggest that anodic protection may have a beneficial effect in the long term by reducing the duration of any subsequent electrolytic conservation treatment post-excavation. Research into this is continuing.

See Plate 19 (colour section, p. ix)

A summary of first-aid treatments

Preparations for recovery from under the water

Large items need support before being raised. On site, storage facilities and reagents must be on hand immediately following recovery. Small items need careful packing.

Initial storage/cleaning

When iron has been recovered it is essential to keep it wet, preferably immersed in water, or under wrappings. A corrosion inhibitor, such as sodium carbonate (washing soda), could be added to the storage water if a conservator so advises.

SUMMARY

Iron

Remember that large concretions and ironwork are best preserved *in situ*. If you intend to raise ironwork long-term conservation must be arranged beforehand.

- Give adequate support to the find before lifting.
- Have all storage solutions and clean storage containers immediately at hand.
- Upon the advice of a conservator place finds in a solution of corrosion inhibitor, if necessary.
- If finds are too large to be totally immersed, wrap them in towelling or plastic foam soaked in corrosion inhibitor. Then seal them in polythene wrappings.
- Watch out for signs of corrosion and seek conservation advice immediately.

Iron displaying phosphate corrosion (sometimes identified as thin layers of dark blue or black corrosion products) needs special attention. Do not store these finds in conditions where they will be exposed to oxygen-rich water. Instead wrap or bag them in polythene which will act as a barrier and then embed them within samples of the deposit from which they came. Fill up the storage containers with water from the site, keep them chilled and in the dark and seek further advice from a conservation laboratory as soon as possible. This should help prevent oxidation of the delicate phosphate layers.

Concretions must neither be removed from finds before conservation, nor broken apart to see what is inside. Not only do they provide valuable protection from corrosion, but they may also hold unknown finds and incidental evidence within. They will require detailed examination before the nature of their contents can be fully determined: too often they are broken open and then discarded as being unimportant because they contain no recognisable find. In other cases the find inside may be damaged and important archaeological evidence associated with it left unrecognised and destroyed. However, concretions can preserve unique and delicate information of all types. X-ray examination is a useful tool to reveal the shape of objects within the concretion, even if the finds themselves no longer exist, and features of ancient use and repair, and surface platings, inlays or other intricate decoration that may be totally hidden within the layers of the concretion itself. They may also reveal the structure and contents of composite artefacts such as instruments and watches. Concretions must therefore be left intact and submitted to a conservator for X-ray examination.

Drying

Iron finds must not be dried. Complete drying cannot be guaranteed and any trapped moisture, in conjunction with dissolved salts, will produce a potent corrosion reagent.

SUMMARY

Concretions

- Keep concretions wet.
- Only X-ray examination can fully determine their contents and the archaeological evidence held within.
- Do not discard, remove or dismantle concretions unless under the direct supervision of a trained and qualified conservator.

Long-term storage

Finds of iron must be stored immersed in corrosion inhibitor, either in tanks, lined crates or even plastic swimming or paddling pools. Small finds can be kept in lidded boxes. There must also be provision for X-ray examination and full treatment in terms of funding and resources. If you cannot guarantee this, finds of iron should not be raised at all.

Copper, bronze, brass

Typical materials

Copper, bronze, brass.

Typical finds

Ingots and scrap metal; cannon, guns and ancient weaponry; tools, instruments and equipment; machinery parts; fittings, wire, bolts, washers etc; containers and cases; coins and tokens; applied surface coatings such as tin-washes or silver platings.

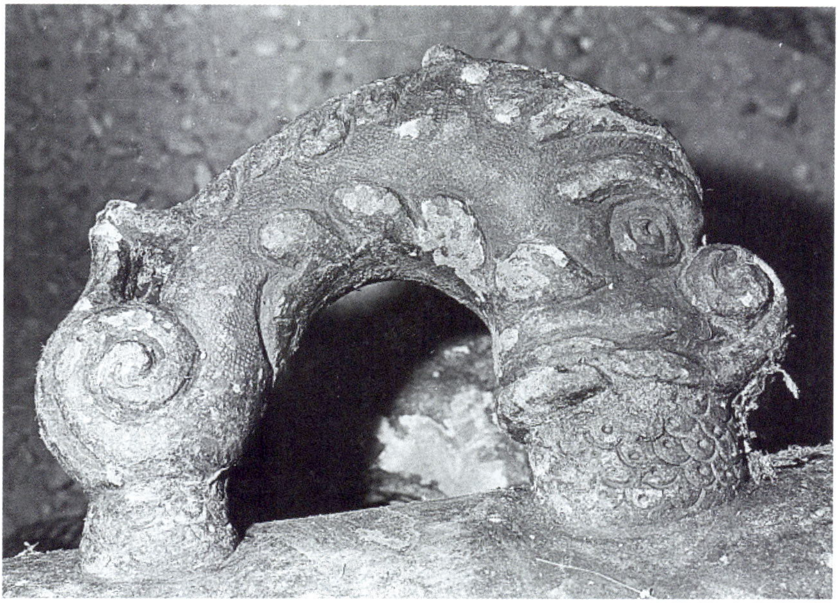

A close-up of the dolphin-shaped lifting lug on a bronze cannon from Charles II's yacht, Mary, *wrecked off Anglesey, 1675. The surface contains fine detail, but has become very soft and easily damaged. (B. Harris)*

Composition and stability

Copper is a pure metal. When alloyed with tin (up to 33%) bronze is formed. Another alloy, gunmetal, was used for weaponry. Now used for valves and steam fittings, gunmetal consists of 88% copper and up to 10% tin, with small amounts of zinc. Copper alloyed with zinc produces brass. Trace elements such as arsenic may also be found in these alloys, together with impurities. Modern coinage is often 'nickel brass'. The metal and its alloys may be cast or annealed, processes that affect the microstructure and that can be revealed by metallographic examination.

Copper and its alloys are comparatively stable in underwater sites. They have often been found in a good condition, although they will start to corrode quickly following excavation.

How copper and its alloys deteriorate

Copper and its alloys often become etched during underwater burial, and this may result in a shiny, pitted surface. More usually the metals form layers of black, red and characteristically green corrosion products. In seawater, surfaces are sometimes found with thin encrustations of marine invertebrates, such as corals, barnacles, ridge worms and hydroids. This suggests that the metal has become stabilised, since the release of copper salts is toxic to most marine organisms (copper compounds are used as the basis of many anti-fouling paints). In anaerobic conditions copper and its alloys do not appear to survive well, with the metals becoming very thin and pitted.

Full conservation treatment

Normal conservation procedures involve treating small items by intensive desalination to extract the chlorides that cause corrosion, followed by one of several different treatments matched to the requirements of the object. Benzotriazole (BTA) was used extensively in the past, but must be used with care as it thought to be cancer-forming.

Large items, like bronze or brass cannon, are sometimes treated by electrolytic reduction.

A summary of first-aid treatments

Initial storage

Copper and its alloys must not be allowed to dry and should be stored immersed in water. If they are too large they should be covered in towelling or other absorbent material and gently hosed down regularly.

Cleaning

You should not attempt to clean copper, bronze or brass. Chemical treatments, although producing good results in the short term, leave corrosive chemicals within the metal that can cause damage later; and wire brushing, which has disfigured many a sound artefact in the past, must be avoided at all costs. Cleaning is best left to a trained conservator with the appropriate skills, knowledge and technical equipment.

Drying

Do not attempt to dry copper and its alloys without the supervision of a qualified conservator.

Long-term storage

Keep finds immersed in clean water, either in boxes, lined crates, baths or paddling/swimming pools. Consult a conservator about the need for chemical corrosion inhibitors.

SUMMARY

Copper, bronze and brass

- Keep large finds wet, immersed in clean water.
- Pack small finds carefully to avoid damage or loss.
- Do not try to clean the find's surface, either with chemicals or by mechanical means, as you may remove information, damage softened surfaces and leave aggressive residues.
- Copper salts are poisonous.

Lead, tin and pewter

Typical materials

Lead, tin and pewter.

Typical finds

Ingots; tableware and cutlery; cladding, piping; amulets, seals, and tokens; ancient anchor stocks; surface coatings of tin on iron or bronze.

See Plate 20 (colour section, p. x)

Composition and stability

Lead is unusual in that it can resist long-term exposure to aerated conditions in seawater, and lead anchors exposed to seawater from Roman times have survived. This is because the metal reacts to form a protective sulphate crust, which inhibits further attack. However, in conditions with low sulphate content, and those which are acidic or anaerobic, the metal is less resilient. It may even react with mildly acidic tap water or soft water. After conservation the metal needs protection from organic acids and vapours coming from cardboard boxes and newspaper, and some adhesives. It is also advisable to wear gloves when handling lead objects, not only to protect your hands, but because acid from the skin may initiate corrosion.

Tin is very reactive and almost certainly will never survive in an uncorroded state. It is typically transformed into a mass of white corrosion products and may well be missed. Sometimes the metal was used as an inlay or overlay, particularly for iron, and remnants of this may be revealed by X-ray examination.

Pewter is an alloy of tin and either lead, in the case of old pewter (lead being used before its poisonous effects were known of), or antimony, possibly with the addition of copper. In underwater conditions pewter usually survives with an uneven warty or pitted surface. In some cases pewter has been found virtually uncorroded.

Full conservation treatment

Apart from tin these metals provide no great problem for conservation unless alloying components and impurities cause complications. They

HEALTH WARNING

Lead, its alloys, compounds and corrosion products are toxic.

When handling lead take the following precautions:

- do not allow the metal or its storage water to come into contact with your skin – wear protective gloves, and overalls if necessary
- wear protective masks if there is a chance you might inhale powdery corrosion products
- wash your hands thoroughly after handling lead or ancient pewter.

are often treated by intensive desalination, or by gentle electrolytic (consolidative) reduction. During storage and display the metals need to be protected from harmful vapours issuing from paints, adhesives, resins and other organic sources such as cardboard boxes, newspapers and wooden shelving.

A summary of first-aid treatments

Preparations for recovery from under the water

Many of these finds are very heavy. Immobilise them before raising and give support to large or heavy objects. Make sure that anyone responsible for handling the finds has been trained in safe lifting techniques.

Initial storage/cleaning

Once they have been recovered these metals should be kept wet, either immersed in water or hosed down and covered by towelling and plastic sheeting.

Working under the supervision of a conservator remove only loose surface debris by spraying or careful brushing. Take great care not to remove impressions of textile or rope, stamps or makers marks. Remember that the surfaces of these metals are soft and lead compounds are toxic. Avoid mechanical or chemical methods of cleaning and take the necessary health and safety precautions.

Long-term storage

Finds must be kept immersed in a slightly alkaline solution. Sea water,

SUMMARY

Lead, tin and pewter

Lead and its corrosion products are toxic. Take care to avoid skin contact when handling leaden finds.

- Keep these finds wet when they have been recovered.
- If it is known that the ordinary water supply is acidic, consult a conservation laboratory on how to make it alkaline. It may be necessary to add sulphate salts, such as sodium sulphate (Glauber's salt) to the storage water.
- Seek conservation advice about the possibility of drying.

hard tap water or alkaline fresh water will do. Soft or acidic water should be made alkaline with the addition of sulphate salts. Obtain conservation advice about this.

Aluminium

Aluminium is the world's third most abundant element and is one of the components of clay (aluminium silicate). It could not be produced as a metal until late in the nineteenth century when the technology had been developed to extract it from its ores.

Typical finds

Aluminium forms many important alloys and its use in the twentieth century is now widespread, although historical finds are still rare. You could nevertheless expect to find examples of modern artwork and statuettes, aircraft parts, aluminium cans, modern machine parts, structural remains and cooking utensils on underwater sites.

Composition and stability

The pure metal itself is extremely reactive but forms a very hard, protective oxide deposit (alumina) which makes it resistant to further attack. Aluminium will corrode if this oxide layer is not allowed to form, or if another metal is present. Duraluminium, containing 4% copper and available since 1908, is harder than the pure metal and more resistant to corrosion in the atmosphere, but less so in seawater. Other metals, such as calcium and magnesium, may be added to make the alloy harder and stronger, and the presence of these metals also reduces its resistance to corrosion.

Full conservation treatment

There are few reported examples of the conservation of aluminium. Work in Australia has shown that the metal corrodes whenever impurities of copper are present, and indicates that successful conservation procedures must involve their removal (Macleod 1983).

A summary of first-aid treatments

Initial storage/cleaning

Immediately on recovery aluminium finds must be kept wet. Natural water can be used. Aluminium is a very reactive metal and will corrode

SUMMARY

Aluminium

Aluminium may be found on modern-day sites.

- Store aluminium finds in isolation from other metals or their corrosion products.
- Keep finds immersed in clean, chilled water.

preferentially when in contact with many other metals, so always store it separately.

On the advice of a conservator loose debris may be removed by careful brushing or hosing.

Precious metals – silver and gold

Typical materials

Pure metals; sterling silver (silver and 7.5% copper); white gold (gold and silver); gold alloy (gold and copper); coinage gold (up to 10 parts silver).

Typical finds

Ingots; inlay, overlay and surface platings; silver plate and silverware; coinage; jewellery.

Composition and corrosion

Silver and its alloys are attacked by sulphides and chlorides and are rarely be found in an uncorroded state. Initially silver alloys may be mistaken for corroded copper, but they are indicated by the presence of white corrosion products that quickly become lilac on exposure to the light. Finds of silver will be very fragile, especially if corrosion has penetrated the crystalline structure of the metal, and silver coinage may be concreted together in a single mass. Ancient silver was sometimes decorated with niello, a black mixture of metallic sulphides.

Gold is an extremely stable metal and the pure form (24 carat gold) does not corrode. Copper or silver present as impurities or alloying metals may do so.

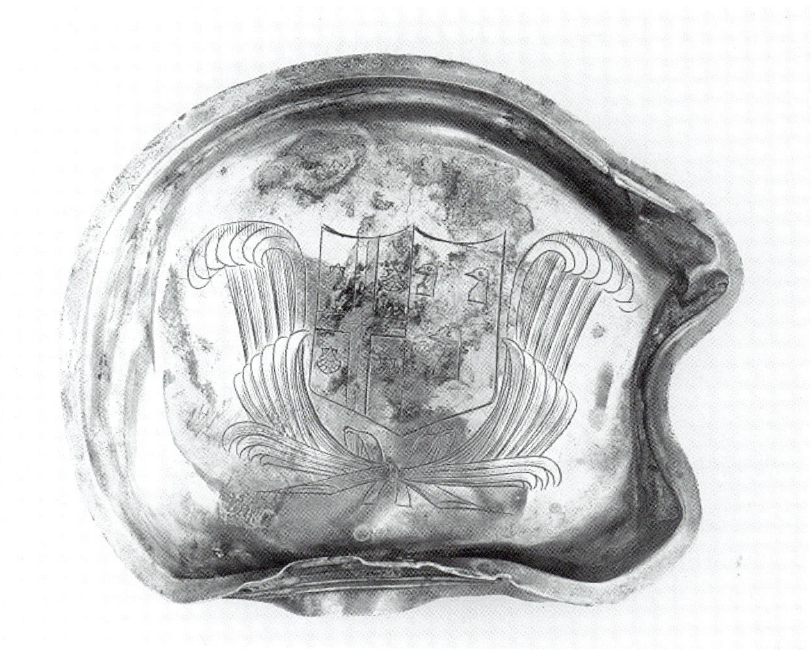

A silver lid from Charles II's Mary. *The finely engraved detail of the surface has been preserved, but the lid has been damaged by the weight of cannon balls that buried it. (B. Harris)*

Full conservation treatment

Precious metals are usually cleaned and conserved by a variety of mechanical methods, chemical treatments or electrolytic reduction. Cleaning and conservation should always be left to a conservator because of the risk of damaging the surface of the metal, and in order to prevent archaeological evidence, such as niello inlays or impressions of other materials, from being destroyed.

A summary of first-aid treatments

Remember that gold and silver finds may have great intrinsic monetary value; apply security measures to prevent them being stolen at any stage of their treatment or during storage.

Preparations for recovery from under the water

Immobilise the finds, pack them carefully and support delicate items. This is especially important for finds of silver that may be highly corroded and severely weakened.

SUMMARY

Gold and silver

Take special security measures to guard against theft.

Pure gold will usually be found in an uncorroded state, although the debased metal may be covered in a variety of corrosion products.

Silver will usually be fragile and badly corroded and may be mistaken for corroded copper.

- Remove finds carefully from under the water.
- Do not attempt to clean these finds.
- Store the finds immersed in clean chilled water.
- Make sure jewellery is carefully packed and take special care with gemstones to prevent them becoming dislodged.

Initial cleaning

Place these finds in water as soon as they are recovered. Do not attempt to clean them in case you damage their softened surfaces, remove surface decoration, or lose gemstones from jewellery.

Drying

Following the advice of a conservator certain finds may be carefully dried after they have been thoroughly desalinated in pure water. Care must be taken with gemstones. Finds containing these are best kept wet.

First-aid storage

Keep these finds immersed in clean water and guard against theft.

6 Stone, ceramics and glass

Stone, ceramics and glass are rigid materials and can be brittle. Finds may occur as the unworked material, such as stone used for ballast, or may be have been made into artefacts such as building blocks, stone shot and crude anchors, sculpture, alabaster containers or ornaments, and the gemstones of jewellery. Manufactured items include ceramics (pottery, porcelain and clay pipes), glass containers and vessels, lenses and window glass. Some artefacts may have been painted or covered with inlays and overlays of precious and semi-precious metals.

See Plate 21 (colour section, p. x)

Survival

These finds will survive on almost any site, although glass may have suffered badly. If protected from the physical processes of destruction (wave action, crushing, shattering, and so on) they may even be unabraded and complete. Fine examples of eleventh-century glass have come from a wreck at Serçe Liman in Turkey (Bass and Van Doorninck 1978). In spite of this, survival for centuries under water is no guarantee that glass will continue to be stable after it has been recovered. Coarse glass, such as that used for green wine bottles, seems to be particularly unstable and should receive special care.

Such finds may also be prone to staining and infiltration by salts, especially the case with porous wares or unglazed ceramics. While staining may be little more than disfiguring, its presence causing no great harm, crystallisation of salts as the find dries can cause great damage.

Full conservation treatment

The conservation of these materials involves many stages. First of all soluble salts must be removed by the process of desalination. You can start this on site by gradually adding clean, non-saline water to storage baths. At some stage encrustations and insoluble salts may be removed,

SUMMARY

Stone, ceramics and glass

These must be protected from:

- accidental abrasion, chipping, fracture and breakage during all stages of excavation, recovery and treatment.
- drying before soluble salts have been removed.

Glass should not dried at all.

carefully and expertly, by a conservator, who will also, if necessary, consolidate the fabric of the find (either before or after drying). Drying will be carried out in the air, or through solvents if surface tensions put the find at risk (glass usually falls into this category). The conservator may then repair the find, with careful selection of adhesives and following a careful restoration plan. After that the find may be put on display, packed for storage or submitted for further analysis.

Stone

Typical materials

Quartz, limestone, marble, alabaster, granite, obsidian (natural glass), sandstone, shales and slate.

Typical finds

Ships ballast, ancient anchors, building blocks, whetstones, millstones, sculpture and carvings, vases and containers, shot, marbles, jewellery, gemstones and amulets.

Composition and stability

These materials come from rocks and minerals and have widely varying chemical compositions. They are classified by geologists as igneous, sedimentary or metamorphic. Minerals are naturally occurring chemical compounds and metal ores of all types.

Classification

Igneous rocks

Examples of igneous rocks include granite, basalt and obsidian (natural glass). These materials were formed when molten material cooled and are in general hard, with a compact non-porous structure. They are basically siliceous and are not infiltrated by soluble salts to the same extent as sedimentary rocks. They form the oldest of the Earth's rocks.

Sedimentary rocks

Examples of sedimentary rocks include sandstone, limestone and shale. These are generally soft and porous materials formed through the sedimentary deposition of individual minerals, shells of marine creatures, and so on, that have become cemented together over aeons. Over long periods of immersion, water is able to penetrate the crystalline structure and damage can occur if any dissolved salts are able to crystallise upon drying.

Metamorphic rocks

Marble, slate and quartzite are metamorphic rocks. They are the result of sedimentary rocks having become recrystallised through the effects of high temperatures and pressures. In general, like igneous rocks, they have a dense structure and are less prone to damage by salt crystallisation than sedimentary rocks.

Minerals

Minerals are pure, or almost pure, chemical compounds that occur naturally, sometimes as crystals. Quartz (in its various forms – chert, flint, rock crystal, rose quartz and amethyst), the minerals of gemstones (diamond, ruby, emerald) and metal ores (haematite, malachite, cassiterite) fall into this category. Some minerals are still ground down and used to form artists pigments (lapis lazuli, limonite, haematite).

How stone deteriorates

The types of stone most susceptible to damage are those with a laminated structure, like shales, or those with high amounts of calcium carbonate (limestone, marble, calcite) or sulphate (alabaster and gypsum). These can suffer variable amounts of softening or pitting, the effects of which will become most apparent on drying. If soluble salts which infiltrated during burial are not removed, they crystallise within the fabric of the stone. The pressures of recrystallisation can cause spalling and destruction of the overlying layers, thus destroying any fine detail that might have been present.

Damage can also be attributed to erosion by water movements, especially if abrasives like sand are present. The grinding or drilling action of marine creatures also causes harm. Marine stone-borers (like the stone piddock, *Pholas* spp.) are the most destructive, with their deep channels penetrating the stone to a depth of several centimetres. They attack shale, sandstone and limestone.

Other types of deterioration are mainly of a disfiguring nature – black, green or rusty stains, or encrustation with barnacles and other marine organisms. These can usually be remedied during conservation.

Full conservation treatment

The conservation of stone involves primarily the removal of salts. This is achieved by soaking finds in changes of fresh water, if necessary distilled or deionised water, until all salts have been removed. This is usually confirmed using a conductivity meter.

Depending on the composition of the stone, stains and encrustations can be removed by a conservator, chemically, mechanically or by a combination of both methods. Repairs can be made using a suitable adhesive.

A summary of first-aid treatments

Initial storage

Following recovery, the risks to the finds are two-fold: damage through crushing or dropping, and damage through drying. Finds need adequate support, and protection from drying. Ideally they should be kept immersed in water, but if they are too large for storage tanks they can be kept wet under hessian or towels and drenched with water at short intervals.

Cleaning

If the surface of the stone is sound a conservator may recommend the careful removal of concretions and encrustations. Cleaning of the surface must stop, however, if you notice any damage being caused. Acid treatments are best avoided, even mild ones, as they may weaken the substrate of the stone and leave harmful residues. Calcite and marble are particularly vulnerable.

Desalination

In a conservation laboratory with the necessary monitoring equipment desalination can be undertaken with continuously running water or changes of water. This is most critical for stone from marine conditions and prior to drying. On site it can be started by adding freshwater to the storage baths.

Drying

It is only safe to dry stone once it has been thoroughly desalinated and following the advice of a conservator. Shale and some sedimentary rocks are best kept wet at all times otherwise they will laminate upon drying.

Long-term storage

Wet finds must be protected from accidental drying before salts have been removed. Store them in sealed containers of clean water. Clean, natural water will suffice until a source of fresh water or tap water becomes available.

Safety note

Sone must always be handled with care. Heavy artefacts can cause crush or strain injuries if not handled correctly. Anyone handling large or heavy items should be properly trained in lifting techniques and

SUMMARY

Stone

Remember to take appropriate safety precautions when handling heavy items.

Limestone, sandstone, shale, marble, alabaster and calcite may have suffered deterioration and need special care. Other types of stone are likely to be more robust.

- Provide adequate support for any large items.
- Under conservation supervision remove loose debris by brushing or spraying with water.
- Store by total immersion in water or by wrapping in water-soaked absorbent material.

equipped with the necessary safety clothing (gloves, steel-capped boots and, perhaps, a hard-hat). Winches and other lifting gear should be made available for very heavy finds.

Ceramics

Typical materials

Low-fired wares: brick, terracotta, earthenware, majolica-ware.

High-fired wares: china, porcelain, stoneware.

Typical finds

Glazed or unglazed tiles, bricks, crockery, table ware, fine china, clay pipes, containers, vases and lamps.

Composition and stability

Low-fired wares (pottery, terracotta and earthenware) are fired below their sinter point (the point at which the clay starts to melt) and will be relatively porous and perhaps soft. High-fired wares (stoneware and porcelain) will have reached the sinter point and will be non-porous and hard. Some finds will be glazed and the stability of the glaze will depend upon its components. Tin and lead glazes tend to be soft and blackened. They may also become detached from the pot body. Glazes formed from salt, sodium or potassium are glassy and more durable.

See Plates 21 and 22 (colour section, pp. x–xi)

How ceramics deteriorate

Penetration of salts is the main cause of deterioration, particularly following recovery. Low-fired wares are especially vulnerable to this. Glazes may react with components in the deposit or water to become stained or crumbly. Physical damage by erosion is another cause of decay, although finds protected from abrasion or water movements may be found in a good state.

Full conservation treatment

Conservation involves the removal of salts and stains, drying and then perhaps repair and, in some cases, restoration.

A summary of first-aid treatments

Preparations for recovery from under the water

Immobilise the object or group of sherds to keep them together and to avoid damage. Try to retrieve all the pieces of a broken and scattered find.

Initial storage/cleaning

It is essential to keep these finds immersed in water to prevent salt crystallisation. Under conservation supervision loosely adherent debris and detritus may be gently rinsed away on site, but only if there is no chance it might contain environmental evidence. Under expert guidance it may be possible to remove concreted material with wooden tools at an early stage, before it dries and hardens, and so becomes very difficult to remove.

At first, store finds in the original source water to prevent the build up of osmotic pressure as the dissolved salts leave the fabric of the find. Replace the storage water daily with increasingly diluted solutions until only pure water or tap water is used.

Desalination

On site, desalination can be started by adding fresh or tap water to storage baths.

Drying

When thorough desalination has taken place and this has been confirmed by a conservator, it may be possible to dry these finds in the atmosphere, without heat.

SUMMARY

Ceramics

- Keep these finds wet until desalination can take place.
- Under conservation supervision remove only very loose debris by careful spraying. Take special care with friable items and deposits that may contain environmental remains.
- Pack finds carefully to avoid abrasion and breakage.

Wet storage

As a first-aid measure keep these finds immersed in clean water and do not allow them to dry.

Glass

Typical finds

Beakers, bottles, beads, lenses, hour glasses, vases and window glass.

Composition and stability

Glass is formed from silica (the glass former), with the addition of glass modifiers and stabilisers. (These are usually the oxides of sodium, potassium, magnesium, aluminium, copper, manganese, calcium or

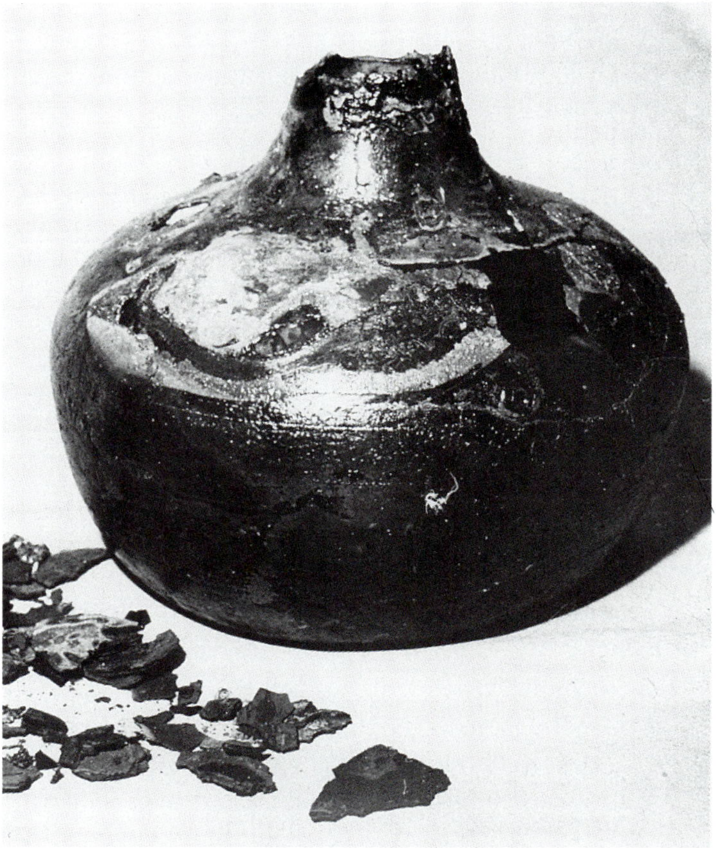

A glass onion bottle from the wreck of HMS Dartmouth *(Sound of Mull, 1690). A hole has formed in the side where the surface of the glass has flaked away. (W. Robinson)*

lead). The presence of other metals gives the glass colour, and may be present naturally (imparting a green hue in the case of iron) or added deliberately (like manganese) to make the glass colourless.

The stability of the glass will depend upon the ratio of the various components. There is no general rule but green bottle glass is usually very unstable.

How glass deteriorates

Glass is a 'super-cooled liquid'. It appears to be solid but the components are still mobile and can easily be leached out. The early stages of leaching cause iridescent rainbow patterns and extreme cases result in exfoliation of the surface. Green bottle glass is particularly prone to this and if allowed to dry, even following desalination, rust-like flakes will peel away like skins from an onion. Other types of glass may resist attack despite centuries of burial.

Full conservation treatment

Because of the unpredictability of the material, conservation of glass presents a challenge and any treatment must only be carried out under expert guidance. Treatments involve desalination, careful drying, perhaps through solvents, consolidation if necessary and repair. To date, there is no standard consolidation treatment and a variety of substances have been tried with varying degrees of success.

A summary of first-aid treatments

Initial storage

In view of the unstable nature of some types of glass and the difficulty in recognising which is which, it is essential to keep all glass wet and totally immersed. Use source water for the storage solution, because tap water may cause osmotic pressures that will further damage the glass.

Cleaning

Do not attempt any cleaning in case the debris contains environmental remains, or the silt you are removing is the means by which a cracked and fragmentary vessel is being held together. Under conservation supervision it may be possible gently to rinse away any surface debris with a fine spray. Stop if there is any risk of damage to the glass or if other remains are found.

Desalination

Do not attempt to undertake desalination unless under the close supervision of a conservator. Glass may start to delaminate during the process and this is irreversible.

Drying

Do not attempt to dry glass unless under the supervision of a conservator: you may cause irreparable damage.

Repair

The repair of glass is a specialist skill and must be left to those trained and qualified.

Long-term storage

Glass must not be dried and should be stored in baths or containers of the natural water. The glass should then be kept in cool or chilled conditions to prevent biological growths. Wrap fragments in bubble-pack to protect them and prevent them piercing the storage bag.

SUMMARY

Glass

- Some glass is stable, some is not. Be careful – only a specialist can distinguish the two.
- Store all glass in baths of the source water (sea, lake, river water) – not fresh or tap water – at chilled temperatures and in the dark.
- Pack all glass carefully to avoid abrasion or breakage.

7 Composite objects and assemblages

This is the most difficult category of find to treat and there are no general rules. It is important to keep composite finds immersed in water, at low temperatures (1°C–4°C) and in the dark. Do not try to take composite objects apart (see Appendix A for further guidance).

Typical materials

Combinations of glass, wood, leather, foodstuffs and metals.

Typical finds

The list of composite objects that may be found on an underwater site is endless, but might include wooden barrels and their contents; cartridge cases in leather bags; iron or bronze guns with wooden carriages; bottles full of wine, corked and sealed with wax; leather boots or belts with brass buckles; decorative pieces of wire bound in fur, and glass flasks bound in wicker-work.

See Plate 23 (colour section, p. xi)

Composition and stability

Composite finds may be found on any underwater site, although the survival of organic material will depend upon enclosure within anaerobic conditions. Despite years of apparent stability this will alter when composites are removed from their burial environment. They may suffer additional damage as the newly exposed components inter-react.

Full conservation treatment

There are no general rules to follow as the preferred treatment for one component might be harmful to the others. An archaeological conservator will need to decide on the best course of action.

SUMMARY

Finds of composite materials

These will commonly occur on underwater sites.

- Do not attempt to clean these finds or dismantle them.
- If possible keep finds immersed in water, at chilled temperatures and in the dark.
- Refer to the Appendix A for further details of storage requirements.

A summary of first-aid treatments

Initial storage/cleaning

Keep these finds wet when they have been recovered. Total immersion is preferred but if finds are too large they must be covered with absorbent materials and regularly drenched, gently, with water. It is important never to let them dry out.

Under conservation supervision remove loose debris by careful brushing with soft brushes or gentle water sprays. Concretions should be left in place.

Long-term storage

The best course of action is to store composite finds immersed in water, at chilled temperatures and in darkened conditions. If this is not possible corrosion inhibitors or biocides may be needed but seek the advice of a conservator before using them.

III

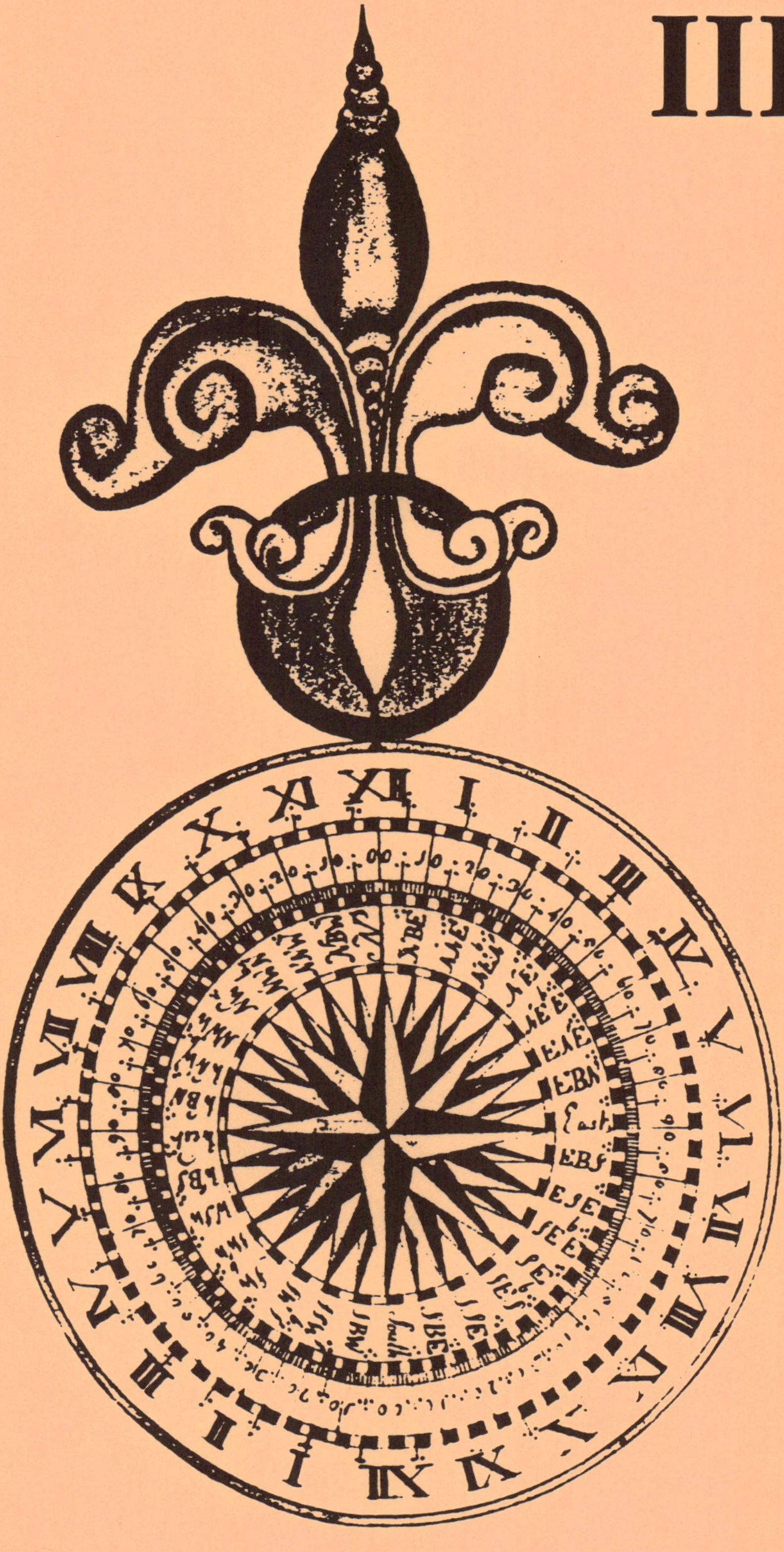

8 First-aid procedures

In most cases, by far the best course of action is to leave objects where they were found. There may be no need to disturb the site – the mere act of discovering a find does not justify its removal, and may herald its destruction. Far better to leave the find alone where natural processes can continue to preserve it. However, in extreme cases and upon expert advice, recovery may be necessary. Finds must then be reported to the appropriate authorities (for example the UK Receiver of Wreck), national or regional heritage bodies must be alerted, and competent archaeological and conservation advice must be sought.

All first-aid treatments need careful planning and expert supervision. This is as important for isolated finds as for when large volumes of material are to be recovered. It means having well defined conservation strategies in place before recovery, and having a source of conservation expertise for guidance during processing (see Chapter 2.) There are four occasions when one must intervene:

- during excavation and recovery
- on the first day of recovery
- at the first-aid premises
- leading to transfer to the conservation laboratory.

During excavation and recovery

During any operation steps must be taken to minimise deterioration as finds become exposed. If they are going to be recovered, you must ensure that they are meticulously recorded, securely packed and carefully raised. These are specialist underwater archaeological techniques and you will require expert training and guidance.

The initial objective will be to minimise exposure of the site while excavating. This is not easy and underwater archaeologists throughout the world are trying to discover the best way of doing this. Several methods have been tried including attempts at redepositing silt, planting natural or artificial sea-grass and covering the site with old tyres, plastic sheeting, sand or gravel. At the Duart Point wreck, off the Island of Mull, Scotland, over 400 sandbags were laid over areas of the wreck in an attempt to restrict erosion (Martin 1995). As yet, there is no standard method and on some occasions all that has been achieved is increased scouring at other parts of the site. Sometimes the removal of only one or two elements of a site can result in massive scouring and erosion of the rest of the area. It is clear that each site requires a detailed and scientific investigation of its water currents, natural deposits and ecosystem before any decision on backfilling can be made.

See Plate 24 (colour section, p. xii)

Preparations before raising

Recording and labelling

Recording and labelling constitute archaeological techniques for which you will need specialist training. The detailed surveying of the site and recording of every find, even isolated ones, with the exact location in relation to the rest of the site or area is essential to preserve the archaeological integrity. You must obtain expert advice before proceeding.

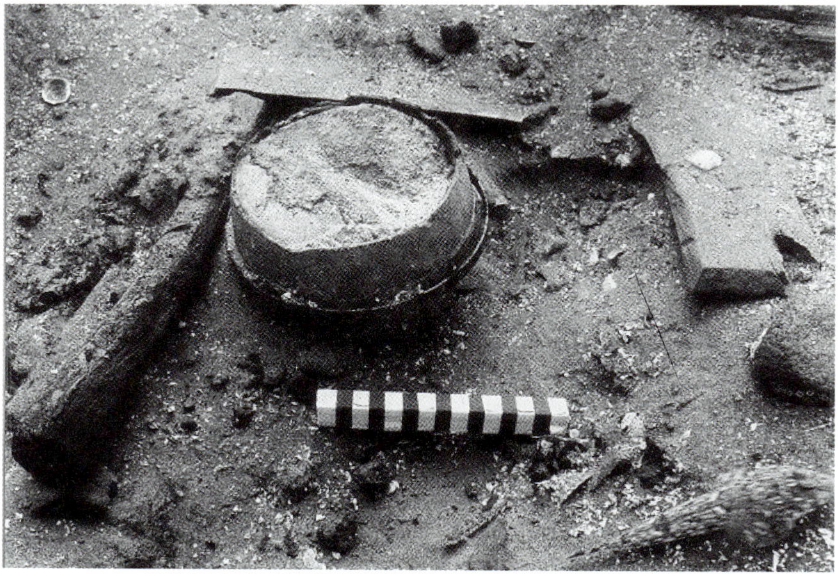

A wooden mariner's compass exposed in situ *during excavations on the wreck site of the Cromwellian warship* Swan *(1653) off Duart Point. It is upside down. The bottom, which shows traces of the instrument's textile covering, has imploded as a result of water pressure on its sealed interior when the ship sank. The brass gimbal ring is still articulated. (C. Martin)*

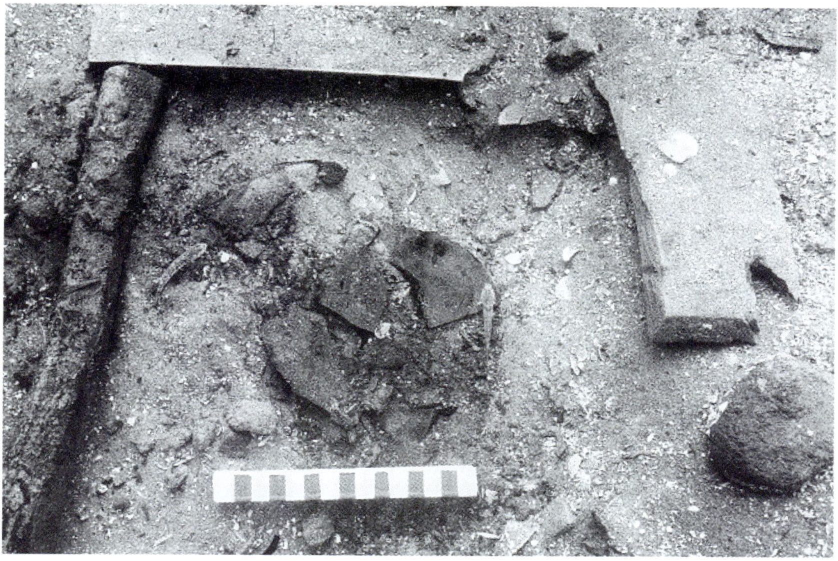

The compass's broken glass face (in an extremely fragile condition), revealed after the removal of the bowl. It had evidently shattered on impact with the seabed. (C. Martin)

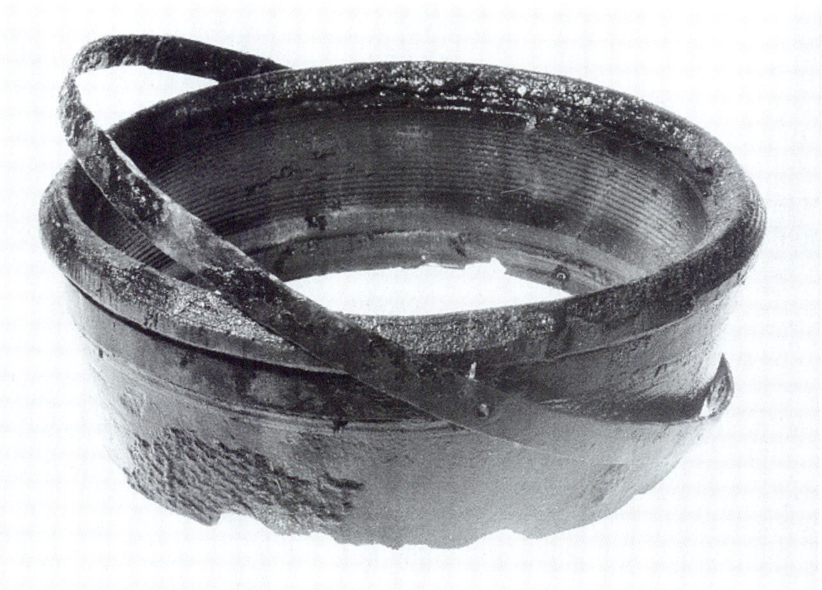

The compass bowl and gimbal ring after the removal of the base. Note the fragment of textile adhering to the outer wall at the lower left. (C. Martin)

At some stage of the operation finds will need identification tags or labels, preferably one inside the storage box or bag and another on the outside. These labels take on a special significance and are the key to the archaeological identity of the find. They must be made of a resilient material, written on with a permanent marker, and must always accompany the find and never be lost. (See page 103 for more details about labels.)

See Plate 25 (colour section, p. xii)

Packing finds before recovery

Packing finds before recovery will once more draw upon specialist expertise and practice – not least to overcome the difficulties of working underwater and to avoid damaging or disturbing nearby archaeological material. Robust small finds should be placed, with an identification label, into polythene bags or containers and then put into larger ones before being taken to the surface. Delicate or flimsy finds will need a firm support and secure covering to immobilise them. Clusters of finds may need to be kept together to preserve their archaeological associations and then excavated and packed accordingly. Individual boxes or containers can then be transferred, with labels, to a crate ready to be carried or raised to the surface with winches.

Large items present additional problems and will need extra support, such as trays, boards, plastic or aluminium mesh, scaffolding or even pairs of step ladders. You will also need plenty of soft padding and wrappings (such as synthetic foam) to cushion the find as it leaves the water, and all bindings, (webbing or plastic strips) must be secure, with precautions to stop them cutting into softened surfaces. Tight bindings of cord or rope in direct contact with the surface of the find will damage it.

Lifting techniques

Lifting underwater finds requires specialist training and techniques, and for large finds may involve outside contractors. Particular care must be taken, for finds are especially vulnerable at this stage: not only do they have to bear their own weight but also that of the water with which they are saturated. As outlined above they must be placed into lifting containers or given rigid support. The support or container can then be manoeuvred and not the find direct. Mechanical lifting methods, for example hoists or winches, should be used instead of relying on the services of a tired, and perhaps cold, diver. With specialist training, excavators may use airbags. Here the ascent must be carefully monitored with the bags vented to prevent the find (and, more seriously, the diver) shooting out of the water like a rocket. On occasion, commercial lifting gear will be necessary and you may need to involve contractors.

(a)

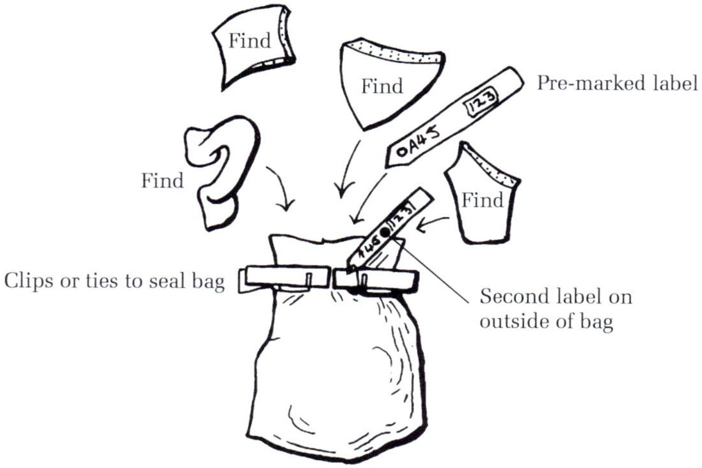

(b)

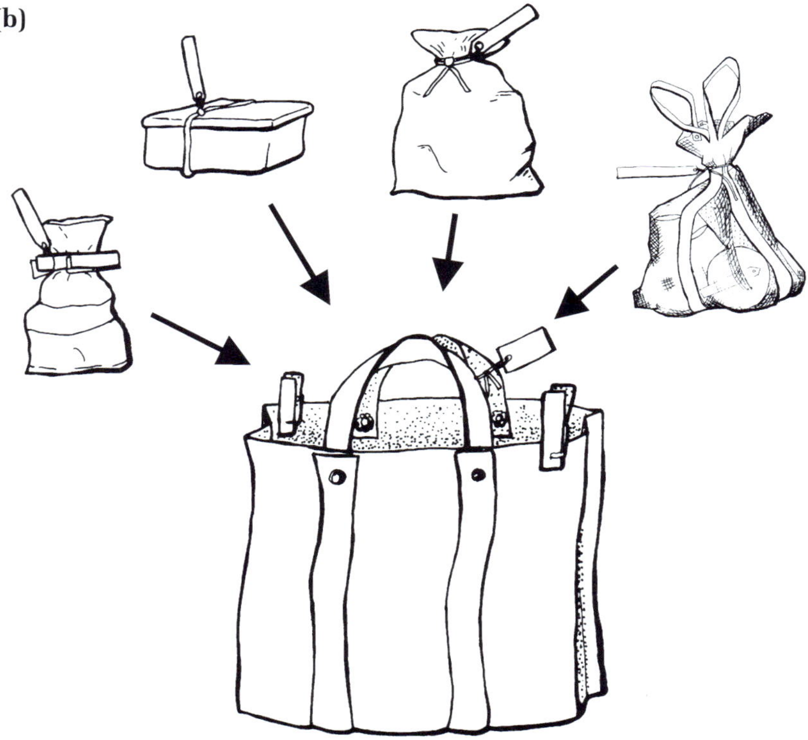

Figure 4 (*a*) *Preparing small finds for raising to the surface – small finds and their labels are first placed inside a polythene or mesh bag.* (*b*) *Preparing small finds for raising to the surface – bagged and boxed small finds are placed in a mesh bag for transportation to the surface.*

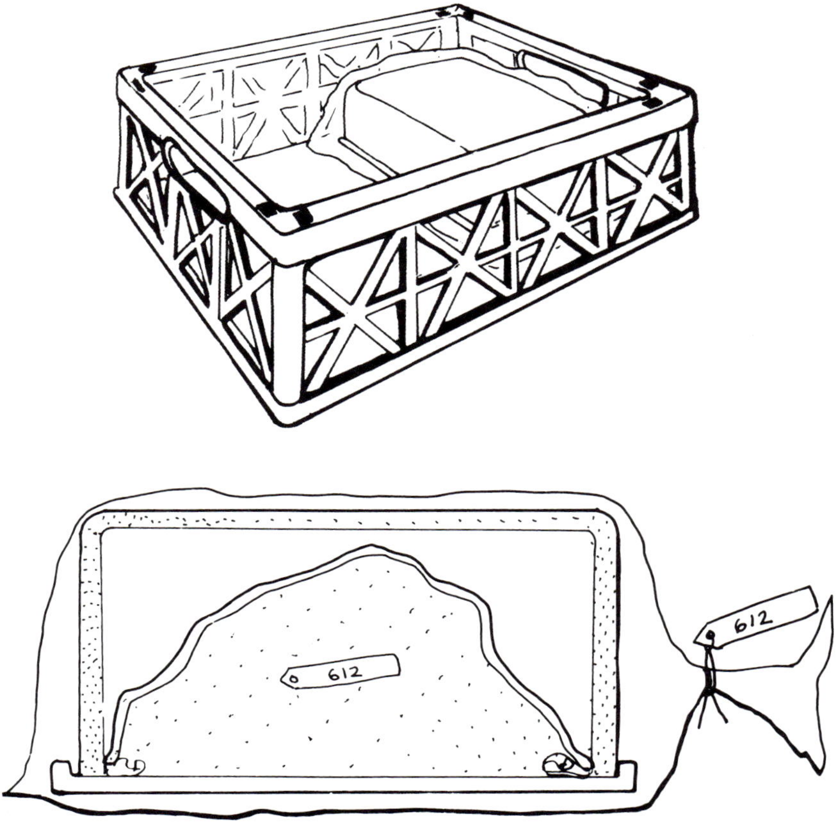

Figure 5 *Preparing large finds for transportation to the surface, boxed and bagged finds are placed in lifting crates before being transported.*

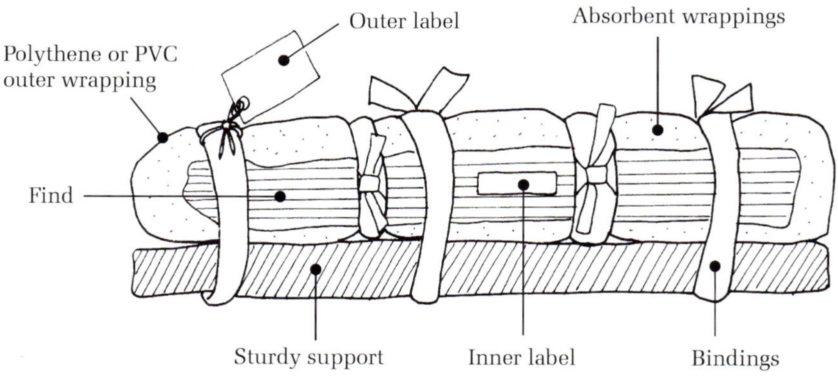

Figure 6 *Very large finds will need to be given sturdy support before being raised.*

When they reach the surface finds should be left as packed and passed immediately to someone especially appointed to take charge. The first objective here is to protect the find from being crushed by exhausted divers or their equipment. Sorting for the next stage of first-aid will then be necessary.

See Plates 26, 27 and 28 (colour section, pp. xiii–xiv)

On the first day of recovery

Following a find's recovery it is important to follow the advice of an archaeological conservator. You will be initially guided on how to minimise the impact of change. Time will be of the essence, for having survived the perilous journey from under water to the atmosphere, the find will be exposed to new agents of physical destruction, chemical alteration or biological decay. These forces will begin to take immediate effect so to prevent this finds must be carefully apportioned to the correct type of holding storage, and then prepared for transportation to the premises where they can receive more permanent first-aid treatment.

On-site storage

During on-site storage the general rule is to keep finds wet (preferably totally submerged), cool and in the dark. No special type of water is required. The source water from which the find came is best and almost any type of container can be used; the ones with close-fitting lids to be preferred. Speed will be of the essence and you will need the expert advice of a conservator.

See Plate 29 (colour section, p. xiv)

Equipment needed

Depending on the quantity and nature of the expected finds you should have at hand some or all of the following:

- an assortment of clean tubs, crates and plastic boxes, of all sizes and with well fitting lids
- insulated cool-boxes or cool-bags containing refrigerated coolant packs (as used in picnic cool-boxes), for the storage of delicate organic finds
- absorbent materials, such as rolls of synthetic sponge, hessian sacks or towelling to wrap or cover large finds that will not fit into storage tanks
- sheets of polythene, PVC, metallised plastic (like mountaineers'

survival blanket) or tarpaulin to cover large finds and their wrappings and to prevent evaporation
- separate holding tanks, pools or storage areas for large ferrous metals and concretions, large non-ferrous metals, inorganic finds, large organic finds and samples (these holding tanks or pools should be filled with samples of the water from which the finds have just come, lidded and placed in the shade or covered to minimise temperature increase)
- a supply of mesh bags, polythene bags, lengths of plastic sheeting, polythene bubble-pack and polyether foam
- a supply of good quality waterproof marker pens and waterproof labels (spun-boned polythene)
- webbing and strips of polythene to use as bindings; lengths of synthetic twine or nylon fishing line to use as ties for bags

Deciding which finds need treatment first

As soon as it is recovered the find must be given a quick examination to appraise its state and condition and to identify material that will require treating first (unstable finds and large or bulky finds). Finds should be dealt with in the following order.

1. Perishable finds Charts, documents or fragments of paper and perishable items must be dealt with immediately. Disturb them as little as possible and place them in cool or chilled conditions – a refrigerator is ideal but a cool-box, of the type used on picnics, will do as an interim measure. Keep them covered and in the shade.

2. Finds too large for crates Awkward finds too large or bulky for any available crate or tank should be left on their original support to assist handling. Until a holding tank of a suitable size can be found they must be protected from the effects of drying by being drenched with water, wrapped in layers of water-absorbent materials and then covered with an impermeable layer that will prevent evaporation. Take care with bindings that may cut into softened surfaces – instead use wide polythene strips or webbing padded around with polyether foam or polythene bubble-pack padding (smooth side to the find). Sustained drenching throughout the day may then be necessary to keep the find wet and cool.

3. Other finds Other finds can be safely stored immersed in tap water or clean source water and kept covered and cool.

Packing for transportation to the first-aid premises

To enable finds to survive the perilous journey to the first-aid premises they must be carefully packed. Keep them in their storage boxes, with plenty of padding between them. Seal the boxes with tightly fitting lids to stop evaporation and spillage, carefully label them and pack them into larger crates and boxes. Prepare them for a bumpy journey, no matter how close the intended destination may be.

Batches of finds should be taken to the first-aid premises without delay: aim for all finds to be transferred by the end of the day's excavation.

See Plate 30 (colour section, p. xv)

At the first-aid premises

The first-aid premises may be a finds hut, workshop, or some other temporary location. Working under expert supervision your objective here will be to stabilise finds until they can receive conservation treatment. First-aid treatments involve minimum intervention and will involve little more than selection of the right type of storage. Any further treatment, such as cleaning, desalination or drying, must only be undertaken under the supervision of a qualified archaeological conservator.

Layout of the workshop

Depending on the size of the operation you will need:

- a dry area for updating records and documentation
- a finds reception area with temporary holding tanks (as on site), for immediate storage
- workbenches for general use
- a water source
- a wet area for examining finds
- wet storage area/tanks
- refrigerators.

If you are working under the guidance of a conservator you may also need:

- desalination tanks
- benches where finds can be dried
- an area for dry storage.

Reception of finds

As soon as finds arrive they must be logged, prioritised and placed in appropriate storage solutions. Here archaeological and conservation practices overlap and neither must interfere with the requirements of the other. To enable prompt and effective first-aid treatment each batch must be dealt with before the next arrives.

Logging

Upon arrival finds will be logged by the archaeologists and allocated a find number to identify the find and its archaeological context. The find number must never be lost or mixed up with another – first-aid treatments and recording processes will need to guard against this. Finds must also have their first-aid treatments recorded with details and dates. This is important information that will be needed to track finds, and may influence decisions later in the conservation process.

Prioritising treatments and storage

As each batch of finds arrives briefly examine it and rescue the most fragile items. Deal with these first.

Perishable items that will deteriorate within minutes

These finds demand immediate treatment and warning should be given beforehand to expect them. All necessary storage equipment should be at hand: minutes matter, and exposure to light or atmospheric conditions may result in irreversible change. These finds will be archival material (documents and charts), or other finds with fugitive dyes, inks or writing or perishable items. Make no attempt to clean, examine or unpack these finds. Instead place them immediately, with their original storage solution, into a cool-bag or a refrigerated area. Do not delay before obtaining further specialist advice.

Finds too large or too bulky for crates

These will usually be large wooden finds, heavy timbers, concretions and iron. They must receive treatment within a half an hour of being received, but you may find that they are too large to be totally submerged in storage baths until new ones can be constructed. They could appear robust but this is deceptive. On the contrary, in an exposed state they are highly unstable.

First check their packaging for any leakage. If all is well keep the finds sealed and in their original packing; otherwise repair or re-pack as necessary. As soon as possible construct a crate or pool large enough to take them. In the case of concretions and ironwork there is the additional risk of corrosion, especially in warm conditions. Obtain the advice of a conservator who may authorise the use of a corrosion inhibitor. Sodium carbonate solution is the one most commonly used.

Finds needing treatment before the end of the day

Flimsy organic material such as leather and textiles, finds made of more than one material (composites) and samples taken for scientific examination fall into this category. They must be dealt with before the end of the day.

Before storing samples you must work closely with the specialist involved: the wrong course of action may invalidate results. You will be guided on the correct course of action, and usually told not to interfere but to keep the sample sealed and wrapped, placed under refrigeration or in darkened, chilled conditions, and kept until it can be collected. Be guided on the need to replace storage water if biological growths occur and take special care to avoid cross-contamination of samples required for radiocarbon dating.

Other finds in this category may also be placed in a refrigerator or kept in darkened, chilled conditions. Disinfectants or biocides must not be used. During long periods of storage monitor solutions weekly and change the water if biological growths occur (early signs are sliminess, colourful changes on the surface of the find or storage solution, fine grain-like deposits or the occurrence of thread-like growths).

Finds that must be treated before the end of a week

These are mainly small finds of wood, lead and pewter that will arrive from the site submerged in baths of water. They must receive first-aid treatment within one week of recovery.

Wooden finds must be placed in a refrigerator or otherwise kept chilled. If this is not possible place them in opaque, lidded baths of water, checked fortnightly and changed if biological growths occur. Running water may also be used.

Lead, unless it is pure, and pewter should not be refrigerated: tin changes its microstructure at temperatures below 14°C and becomes granular (although these changes may already have taken place before the find was recovered). Place them instead into baths of clean alkaline ('hard') water. If the water is acidic, or 'soft', add a little sodium sulphate.

Finds that need treating before the end of fortnight

If kept undisturbed following recovery, provided that they are kept submerged in water, certain of these finds should be stable for up to a fortnight. They comprise finds of bone or ivory, copper and its alloys, aluminium, tin and precious metals. Before the end of this period they should be transferred into baths of clean water and checked again at fortnightly intervals. Any additional treatment must only be undertaken by a qualified conservator.

If you have large quantities of animal bones you will need advice from a bone specialist on how to deal with them. You may then be advised to start desalination, followed by drying, but only undertake this under the supervision of a qualified conservator.

Other finds, including ceramics, stone and glass will also remain stable for long periods provided the whole find is immersed and undisturbed. Containers must be sealed to prevent evaporation. Particular care is needed with glass and any porous material. Keep them all totally submerged: any objects protruding through the surface of the water may act as a 'wick', drawing up salts and stains into the exposed area. Apart from regularly checking the level and condition of the storage water, replacing it when it becomes contaminated, little more than protecting the finds from abrasion and physical damage will be needed. For glass, samples of the original source water, not tap water, must be used for storage, but this is not necessary for ceramics or stone. On conservation advice it may be possible to start desalination.

Long-term continuous spraying

On massive finds, such as hull structures, first-aid may involve using a water spray system. This will be a major undertaking and must only be done under the supervision of a qualified conservator who knows the health risks involved. Chilled water will be essential, not just to protect the find but to minimise potential health risks, not least those caused by the deadly bacterium responsible for Legionnaire's disease, *Legionella pneumophilia*, which flourishes at temperatures above 20°C.

Packaging

(For details of storage solutions see the Quick Guide in Appendix A.) If possible keep finds in the crates or boxes in which they were raised. This will prevent unnecessary disturbance. On the *Mary Rose*, as more and more material was being discovered packed in their original barrels, chests and boxes, a method was developed whereby simple, but strong, wooden crates were designed and fabricated to the dimensions of each individual chest or barrel. The entire find was then placed in the new wooden crate, which was lined and padded as required with sheets of polythene. Above water, archaeologists were then able to recover all of the material from each, and found plum stones, peppercorns and other small items that might otherwise have been lost.

See Plate 31 (colour section, p. xv)

In some circumstances and on archaeological and conservation advice it may be necessary to re-pack finds. This will be important if the packing has become contaminated, the storage water needs changing, storage is going to be long term or the finds are to be transported to another location.

Bags and boxes

The advantage of using bags and boxes is that finds can be kept immersed in storage solution. Polythene bags, preferably of the self-seal type with a white strip for labelling, and boxes with air-tight lids can be bought in different sizes, or bags may be made with heavy duty polythene and a heat sealer. Careful matching of the size of the container to the size of the find is important. This will serve to immobilise the find, limit the amount of oxygen that can dissolve and restrict damage caused by abrasion. If heat-sealing is being used, seal together a double layer of polythene as a precaution against leakage, and double seal to ensure an effective weld along all edges.

When adding storage solution try to eliminate any air above the surface, either by filling to the brim, covering the surface with a floating layer of polythene sheeting or with small spherical beads. Polythene bags may be sealed underwater to eliminate air. This will prevent oxygen dissolving into solution and causing damage.

Labels must always accompany the finds. Place them directly with the find inside the bag or container. If any other chemicals, such as corrosion inhibitors, have been added, place an additional label with the name and strength of solution in with the find. Complete details of labels should also be written on the outside of the bags, since even with the best efforts, details (even a single character) on an internal label can become illegible. Place batches of the same type and size of find, individually wrapped, into storage boxes.

Fragile finds, or finds with sharp edges, may first need to be wrapped in bubble pack, or supported between layers of polyether foam, polyethylene foam or synthetic mesh. Aim to keep any two-dimensional material, such as strips of leather or textile, flat.

Bulky or three-dimensional finds may be packed directly into plastic boxes with well fitting lids. Some items may need packing with polyether or polyethylene foam to immobilise them and to protect any delicate areas.

Very large finds, such as timbers, ironwork or concretions, will need custom-built tanks. These can be constructed from wood or scaffolding with reinforced joints and sides to take the weight of the water they will contain. They should be lined with heavy duty PVC or polythene, of the type used to line ponds or paddling pools, and be constructed with a well fitting lid. Line the tanks with bubble-pack, polyether or polyethylene foam padding to prevent the finds from puncturing the plastic and if possible make them manoeuvrable by building them onto a metal frame (eg Dexion) with castors. Place the find onto a support and then cradle it in a strong plastic or webbing sling before putting it into the tank. This will facilitate lifting later.

At some sites outdoor pools (old swimming pools or ponds constructed from dug-out hollows lined with heavy duty plastic) can been used as temporary storage for large timbers. These must be covered by opaque plastic with a reflective surface to prevent heat accumulation and evaporation, and the storage water must be changed regularly or flowing water used.

See Plate 32 (colour section, p. xvi)

Wrappings

An alternative to total immersion is wrapping and sealing. Large finds, such as ships timbers, where total immersion may be impractical, should be wrapped in absorbent material (such as polyether foam, hessian or towelling), soaked in fresh or tap water and completely encapsulated between two or more layers of heavy duty polythene. Where there is a risk of insect attack, sheeting of laminated metallised polyester/polythene (such as that manufactured by Rexam, similar to mountaineers' silvery survival blankets) should be used. A label should be placed between the two layers and another on the outside, and the ends of the package should be sealed with a heat sealer or firmly secured with aluminium or insulating tape or cable ties. They should then be stored somewhere cool, in the dark, away from any threat of insect or rodent damage and checked every 3–6 months for evaporation and possible animal attack.

Cleaning

Cleaning must not be attempted by the non-specialist. Over-zealous cleaning not only causes damage by removing protective coverings, but may inadvertently remove important archaeological or environmental evidence, such plant or food remains, or marks of wear or repair that testify to the find's use. Removal of corrosion products may, in addition, destroy evidence of surface coatings, such as paint or gilding held between layers of corrosion, or may strip away what was the original surface of the metal itself. Concretions, crusts or corrosion products should not be removed as they are protective and may hold evidence of organic material that has since perished, such as woven fibres or the impression of lace. Power tools and wire brushes must never be used.

Chemical stripping also risks leaving residues that cause damage later on, or may form bubbles or may generate heat that may weaken a damaged or friable surface.

Any attempts to clean finds, whether chemically or mechanically, are interventionist techniques and must only be undertaken following training and under the direct supervision of a qualified conservator.

See Plate 33 (colour section, p. xvi)

Desalination

The thorough removal of salts – desalination – is an essential process before any marine find can be dried, but it is another interventionist technique that must be carried out only under supervision of a conservator. It requires copious supplies of clean, fresh water and careful handling and can be a lengthy process where the end-point must be carefully monitored and scientifically recorded.

Dealing with concretions

Concretions are characteristic features of marine sites where iron is present. They are hard amorphous lumps but have a special significance because within them may be preserved rare and delicate finds. Some concretions, particularly those on cast iron, may hold remains of the find itself, albeit in a fragile state. Others, for example those made from wrought iron or steel, may hold a hollow cavity replicating in fine detail the shape of the artefact long perished. Others still may embed organic material or its remains. There is no way of knowing what a concretion may hold until it has been examined by gamma or x-radiography. Under no circumstances should a concretion be discarded or cracked open to see what it contains until it has been examined by an expert: to do so may destroy these important remains. Never discard even the smallest concretion.

Storage

On close examination it is sometimes possible to make out finds embedded within the concretion or to recognise impressions of lost material. Examine concretions carefully and store them according to the following types:

- concretions with residual iron that can be detected by a magnet (see below)
- concretions known to contain embedded non-ferrous finds
- concretions with no embedded finds visible

Concreted marine iron is highly unstable and should not be removed from the seabed, but sometimes small concretions with residual iron that can be detected by a magnet are recovered. These require close monitoring. After being raised they may quickly react to generate heat and this further speeds up the process of decomposition. They may then fall apart with dramatic effect. Pay special attention to these. Keep them covered and cool at all times. Watch for small bubbles coming from the surface. These indicate that active corrosion is taking place and a conservator must be consulted for advice on the corrosion inhibitor to be used. Sodium carbonate solution (washing soda) is the commonest inhibitor used (see Appendix A).

If a concretion is seen to hold embedded finds, it should be kept immersed in chilled water, without chemical additives, and stored in the dark. Under no circumstances must the concretion be allowed to dry, and never attempt to extract the embedded finds. Careful packaging and immobilisation may also be needed to prevent the weighty concretion damaging any fragile finds protruding through the surface.

Even if there are no embedded objects visible, keep the concretion totally immersed in water. Check the concretion regularly and if it appears to be cracking or releasing bubbles contact a conservator who may advise you to add a corrosion inhibitor.

Drying

Drying is an interventionist technique and must not be carried out other than on the advice of a conservator.

Preparing for transfer to the conservation laboratory

The objective of this stage is to finalise first-aid documentation and pack finds so that they will withstand the journey to the conservation laboratory. Prepare finds for the worst possible journey: imagine what would happen to the find if it were dropped and ensure the packaging used guards against this.

See Plate 34 (colour section, p. xvi)

There are certain procedures to follow.

- First check all finds for biological activity and if necessary replace the storage solutions.
- Check also for leakage. Re-pack the finds if required and make sure that seals are intact and that lids are firmly in place.
- Check that labels are legible and accurate and that all documentation is complete. Attach a label to crates or containers listing their

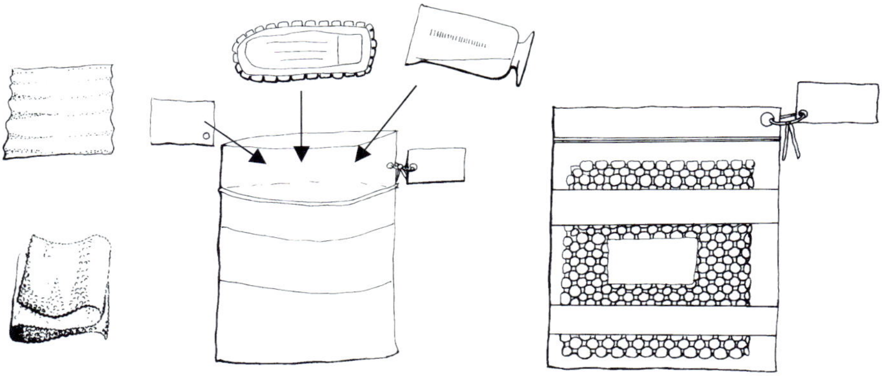

1. Finds are wrapped in bubble-pack and placed in polythene bags.

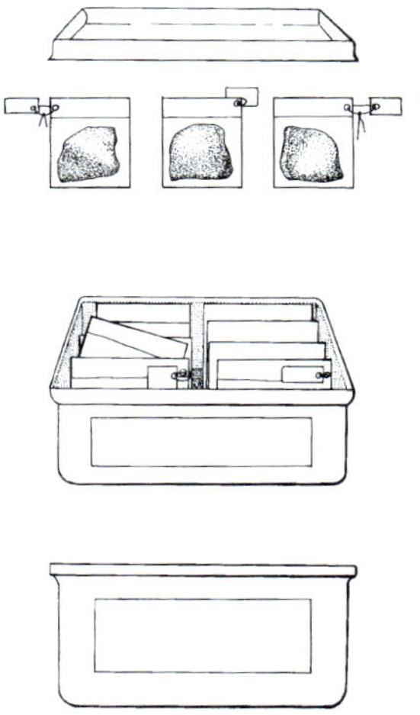

2. Bagged finds are placed in storage boxes.

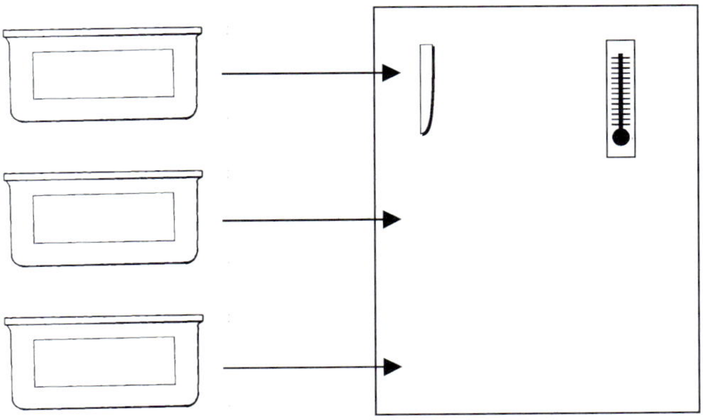

3. Boxes are stored in a refrigerator.

Figure 7 *Finds wrapped, packed and boxed before being stored in a refrigerator.*

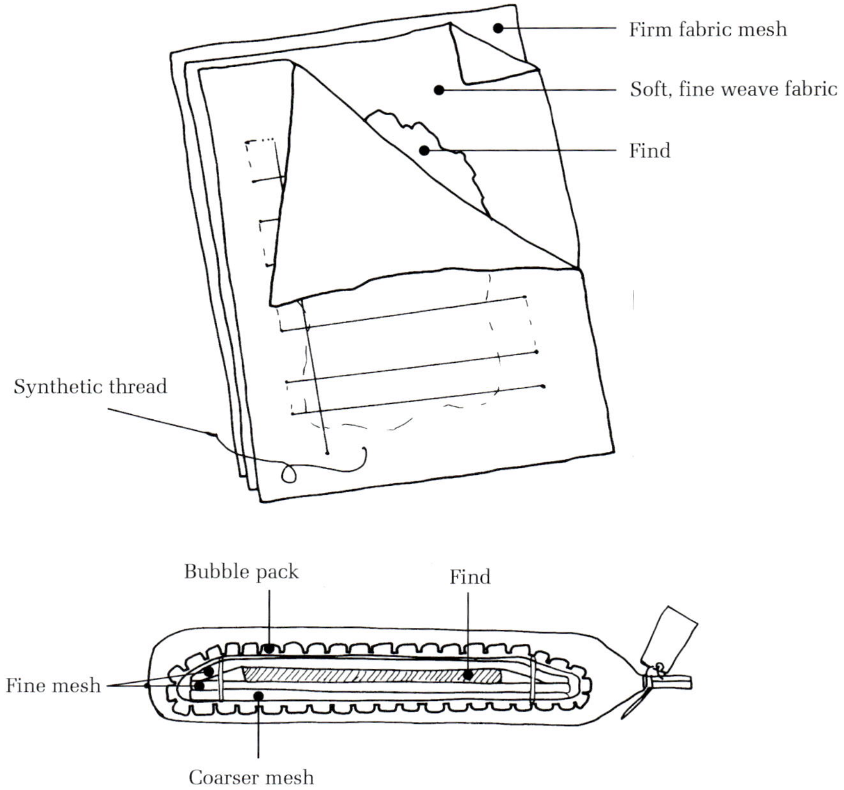

Figure 8 *A fragile, flat find being packed for transportation.*

contents, perhaps colour coding them according to their degree of instability.

- Ensure that bagged finds are immobilised and will not be crushed or damaged by other finds, even if dropped.
- Flat finds should be kept flat with nothing lying directly on top of them.
- Make sure that all finds are immobilised within their storage boxes, trays or crates so that they cannot be damaged. Use extra packaging, such as polystyrene chips, to immobilise small containers held in larger crates.
- Delicate organic material should be placed in cool-boxes or transported under refrigeration.

Other things to consider

Documentation

Keeping accurate and up-to-date documentation is part of the first-aid process and includes the correct logging and labelling of finds, and maintaining a record of the first-aid treatment. A good-quality hard-backed book should be used from the start to record details of containers, together with dates and times at which storage solutions were changed, and so on. To make entries an archival pen, and not a pencil, biro or pen with water-soluble ink, should be used.

Tags and labels

Labels, tags and marking ink must be resilient to long periods of wetting and staining, and must not damage the find. Spun-bonded polyethylene fibre labels are best and are least affected by long-term storage, solvents, heat or light. Dark, embossed plastic Dymo labels or white gardening tags are acceptable for short-term use. The ink used to mark the label should be waterproof and resilient. Black, waterproof ink markers (such as those made by Artline or Staedler), are effective. Do not use pencil lead to mark labels as it will become illegible over time.

If possible secure labels to the find using an inert twine or binding. Metal staples will corrode and natural fibres such as cotton thread will rot, but synthetic materials such as PVC or polythene are suitable. Nylon fishing line, plastic tape and plastic coated metal bag ties could also be used. Whichever method is used the label must be firmly, but not tightly, attached.

If the find is too fragile or an awkward shape, place the label together with the find inside its packaging. In every case a second label should be secured to its outer packaging but avoid writing the label details directly onto plastic containers as confusion will arise if the find and the container become separated. Labels are best secured to large timbers using dipped galvanised or copper nails, or stainless steel pins. Clipper staplers and tacking guns with non-rusting staples could also be used. Avoid non-galvanised iron or iron staples, pins or nails, which will soon corrode.

Finds and samples that are double-bagged should have a label between the two layers.

During long-term storage, record the number and a brief description of the finds held in each tank, box, crate, refrigerator and so on, with the date the find went in and when it was removed. This will help you to locate one find without unnecessarily disturbing the others.

Records of treatments

You must keep full records for each find, perhaps with a sketch or photograph. Liaise with the finds specialist and on the treatment record sheet record the following details:

- archaeological details and a description of the find
- the site number, context number and unique identification number of the find
- the date of excavation
- a description of the find – what it is and what it is made from
- the condition of the find
- its dimensions
- a small sketch or photograph of the find
- any associations (eg 'may be part of find 123')
- any important notes (eg required for radiocarbon dating)
- notes relating to the examination of the find (eg a cross-reference to a drawing or x-ray, notes of any special markings or features)
- conservation details, with dates and signatures to ensure the find can be tracked
- the date the find reached the first-aid workshop and when it left
- details of the treatment it received and the dates when each stage took place
- details of the find's current storage location (eg Refrigerator number 3; Storage tank number 2; Shelf number 6)

On despatch to the conservation laboratory a copy of the first-aid record should accompany the find.

Security issues

Security issues are also part of the first-aid process, and there are several threats you need to guard against, such as wanton acts of vandalism, natural disasters (such as storms or flooding), theft, burglary or sabotage. Never overlook the fact that the greatest threat may come from people working within an operation: prepare for the worst and trust nothing and no one. Always keep your paperwork up-to-date, with signatures, and house it in a secure location, such as a lockable fire-proof cabinet. Make sure your workshop or storage premises are structurally sound and weather-proof, and could withstand the most severe storm. (Choose a location that will not be inundated by spring tides or rivers in flood or will collapse in a gale.) Fix burglar alarms to the building, bars at windows and security lighting outside, and place security locks on doors leading to storage rooms. Choose volunteers carefully, especially if you have never met them before. And remember to protect your computer, and back up any data files held on it.

Health and safety

The health and safety of the finds team is essential. If you employ your work-force you will be bound by current legislation. Advice may be obtained from the Health and Safety Executive who produce a series of excellent pamphlets on safe working conditions and there are a few rules you can observe. Most are common sense.

- NEVER allow food, drink or animals into the workshop.
- Ban smoking.
- The first-aid workshop is not a place for young children who could easily fall into a storage tank and drown. Ensure that risky areas are understood to be out of bounds.
- Make sure that all members of the team and helpers are trained in lifting techniques and are aware of dangers – tubs or water can be very heavy and trying to move them has caused many a back injury or torn ligament.
- Provide safety gear, such as goggles, protective gloves, overalls, waterproof aprons and sturdy boots, and make sure that helpers use them appropriately.
- Keep the workshop clean and, if possible, dry and well ventilated to minimise risks from mould growth and spores.
- Mop up water spillage on floors to prevent them becoming slippery.
- Try to avoid the use of chemicals, but store those that are used, for example corrosion inhibitors, in well labelled containers and always label any solutions you make up. Wear safety goggles, gloves and protective clothing when making up solutions, and dust masks to prevent inhalation of any powder. Remember that they sometimes generate heat when being dissolved in water, so be aware of this, and dispose of wastes very carefully.
- Keep full, eye-wash bottles nearby for use in the event of splashes.
- Special care will be needed when handling lead, which is poisonous. Only handle it when wearing gloves.
- Make sure any electrical equipment, such as computers, lights, deionisers or refrigerators are checked for safety and have the correct fuses in their plugs. Do not overload sockets. Do not permit electrical wires to trail where they may be tripped over or fall into a water storage tank. The combination of water and electricity can be deadly.

Most of this is simply good housekeeping but take nothing for granted. Appoint someone, perhaps on a roster, to take daily charge of keeping the workshop clean, in good order and safe.

Finally, develop a code of practice for your workshop and make all helpers agree to it. Place it on clear view on the walls of the workshop so that it cannot be ignored. It is in everyone's interest for it to be followed.

IV

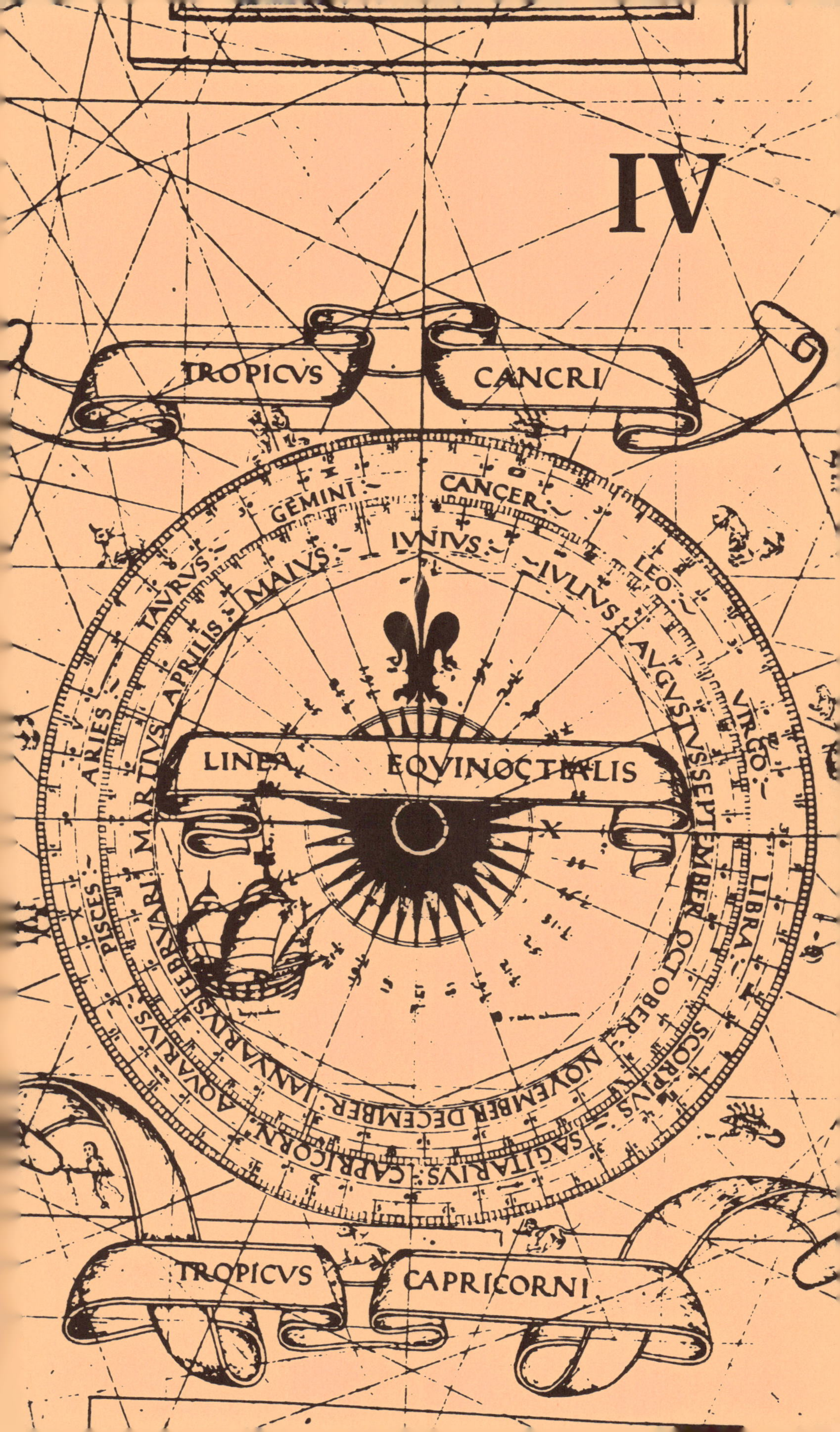
TROPICUS CANCRI
GEMINI
CANCER
TAURUS
IUNIUS
LEO
MAIUS
IULIUS
APRILIS
AUGUSTUS
ARIES
VIRGO
MARTIUS
SEPTEMBER
LINEA EQUINOCTIALIS
LIBRA
PISCES
FEBRUARI
OCTOBER
AQUARIUS
IANUARIUS
NOVEMBER
SCORPIUS
DECEMBER
CAPRICORN
SAGITTARIUS
TROPICUS CAPRICORNI

Appendix A

Quick guide to preliminary storage

The aim of preliminary storage is to maintain the find in a stable state until it can receive conservation treatment. In general terms this means keeping the find

- immersed in water
- cool or refrigerated
- covered or in the dark.

Tables 1 and 2 are guides to preliminary storage. You must monitor the condition of the finds and replace the storage solution with clean water whenever it gets dirty or biological growths occur. Composite finds are very difficult to treat as the preferred storage solution for one component may be harmful to the others. If in doubt keep the find immersed in water, at low temperatures and in the dark. For further advice you must always consult a conservator.

See Tables 1 and 2 (pp. 110 and 111)

Key to storage solutions

Sodium carbonate (washing soda) – corrosion inhibitor for iron

50g sodium carbonate dissolved in each litre of deionised water if available, or fresh water.

Slightly alkaline deionised water – storage solution for lead

1g to 3g sodium sulphate (Glauber's salt) dissolved in each litre of water.

Table 1 Quick guide to the preliminary storage of finds made of only one material

Wood or other organic material	Copper, bronze, brass; silver and gold; aluminium; lead, tin and pewter	Ferrous metals and concretions	Glass, stone and ceramics
Never allow to dry. Store by immersion in chilled water, changed if biological growths occur. Refrigerate, or keep large finds in flowing water. Consult a conservator for advice if finds deteriorate. Investigate IR photography for evidence of writing.	Never allow to dry. Store by immersion in chilled water. Keep cool and covered. For lead, storage water must be slightly alkaline – add sodium sulphate (Glauber's salt) if necessary. Seek conservation advice if finds deteriorate.	Never allow to dry – even large finds. Do not remove or break up concretions. Store by immersion in water – keep cool and covered. Keep large finds covered and totally saturated Seek conservation advice about using sodium carbonate solution as a corrosion inhibitor. Investigate the possibility of X-raying.	Never allow to dry. Store by immersion in chilled water. Keep cool and covered For glass – use the water from which the find came (not tap water). Change the water if biological growths occur. Protect finds from abrasion. Seek conservation advice if finds deteriorate.

Key to terms used in Tables 1 and 2

immersion: Find must be kept wet, by immersion if possible or by covering the find with absorbent material saturated in the storage solution, and sealed in polythene or placed in an airtight container.

X-ray: Examination by X-ray required

refrigerate: Keep the find cool or refrigerated at a temperature between 1°C and 4°C.

Stop! Add no chemical unless so advised by a conservator. Keep the find cool and in the dark.

IR: Photograph on infra-red photographic film.

Table 2 Quick guide to the preliminary storage of finds comprising more than one material

	SECONDARY MATERIAL (for organic materials required for dating or analysis **Stop!**)					
PRIMARY MATERIAL	Wood or other organic material	Copper, bronze, brass; gold and silver	Aluminium	Lead and pewter	Ferrous metals and concretions	Glass, stone and ceramics
Organic material	Store in chilled water: change the water if biological growths occur. Refrigerate if possible. Keep containers covered and in the dark. Seek conservation advice before using biocides. Investigate the use of IR photography.		Store in chilled water, changed if biological growths occur. Refrigerate if possible. Keep finds covered and in the dark. Seek conservation advice if finds deteriorate.	Store in chilled water, changed if biological growths occur. Use alkaline water – add Glauber's salt (sodium sulphate) if necessary. Refrigerate if possible. Keep finds covered and in the dark. Seek conservation advice if finds deteriorate.	Do not remove or damage concretions. Store in chilled water, changed if biological growths occur. Refrigerate if possible. Keep finds covered and in the dark. Seek conservation advice if finds deteriorate. Investigate the use of X-ray examination.	Never allow to dry. Store by immersion in chilled water. Keep cool and covered. Refrigerate if possible. For glass – use the water from which the find came (not tap water). Change the water if biological growths occur. Protect finds from abrasion. Seek conservation advice if finds deteriorate.
Metals Glass Stone Ceramics	Store in chilled water: change the water if biological growths occur. Refrigerate if possible. Keep containers covered and in the dark. Seek conservation advice before using biocides. Investigate the use of IR photography.	Do not remove or damage concretions. Store in chilled water. Refrigerate if possible. Keep finds covered and in the dark. Seek conservation advice if finds deteriorate. For concretions, investigate the use of X-ray examination.				Never allow to dry. Store by immersion in chilled water. Keep cool and covered For glass – use the water from which the find came (not tap water). Change the water if biological growths occur. Protect finds from abrasion. Seek conservation advice if finds deteriorate.

HEALTH AND SAFETY NOTE

Chemicals can be dangerous

The following safety precautions must be observed.

- When mixing up chemicals take care to avoid spillage.
- Wear protective clothing such as plastic gloves, goggles and overalls.
- Avoid any skin contact and wash off any splashes of solution or powder immediately.
- Keep an eye-wash bottle filled with clean water always at hand.
- Some powders release heat when they are mixed in large quantities with water. Take care.
- Keep solutions in well-marked containers warning of the dangers.
- Dispose of waste chemicals safely with copious amounts of water.
- Include with the finds a label indicating the storage solution you have used, the date, and any safety warnings.
- Seek advice on health and safety and statutory requirements. In the UK contact the Health and Safety Executive Information Centre, Broad Lane, Sheffield, S3 7HQ

Appendix B

List of suppliers

General items, including packing materials, plastic storage boxes and chemicals may be obtained from hardware stores, DIY and garden centres, retail chemists and hobby or model shops.

For specialist conservation materials and equipment contact:

Conservation Resources
Unit 1, 2 and 4
Pony Road
Horspath Industrial Estate
Cowley
Oxfordshire OX4 2RD
Tel: 01865 747 755
Fax: 01865 747 035

Preservation Equipment Ltd
Church Road
Shelfanger
Diss
Norfolk IP22 2DG
Tel: 01379 651 527
Fax: 01379 650 582

For suppliers of metallised plastic laminates contact:

Bartec, Paper and Packaging Ltd
50 Wilton Street
Denton
Manchester M34 3NE
Tel: 0161 336 6941
Fax: 0161 336 3030

Rexam Metallising Ltd
Burrel Way
Thetford
Norfolk IP24 3QY
Tel: 01842 755 021
Fax: 01842 762 424

Try also camping specialists for survival blankets made from metallised plastic.

For chemicals and addresses of local suppliers contact:

Merk Ltd
Merk House
Poole
Dorset BH15 1TD
Tel: 01202 669 700
Fax: 01202 665 599

Appendix C

The main wrecks and sites mentioned in the text

Amsterdam, 1749
Merchant ship of the Dutch East India Company, buried in sands at low water mark, Hastings.

Batavia, 1629
Well preserved merchant ship of the Dutch East India Company, wrecked off Western Australia.

Cape Gelidonya wreck, Bronze Age
Hull remains of a cargo ship transporting copper and tin ingots, found off the coast of Turkey.

HMS *Dartmouth,* 1690
British frigate, Sound of Mull, Scotland.

Kennemerland, 1664
Scattered remains of the merchant ship of the Dutch East India Company, wrecked off the Shetland Islands.

John Preston, the 'slate wreck', 19th century
Boat containing a cargo of slate, wrecked near Lochaline, Sound of Mull.

Llangorse Crannog, 9th–10th centuries
Submerged, dark age lake settlement in Wales.

Magor Pill boat, 12th century
A clinker-built vessel initially discovered in the bed of the River Severn, offshore from Magor Pill. The vessel was recovered and is now being conserved by York Archaeological Trust.

Mary, 1675
Charles II's royal yacht, wrecked off Anglesey.

Mary Rose, *1545*
Henry VIII's warship, recovered from the Solent and now on display in Portsmouth.

Randello wreck, Roman
Scattered remains of a cargo ship, Randello, Sicily.

Santo Antonio De Tanna, Mombasa wreck, 1667
Portuguese frigate, wrecked off Mombasa, Kenya.

Serçe Liman wreck, 11th century
Wreck with a cargo of glass found off the coast of Turkey.

Swan, Duart Point wreck, Cromwellian, possibly 1653
Wrecked at the foot of the cliffs, Duart Point, Mull, Scotland.

Wasa, 1628
Well preserved warship found in the Baltic. Raised and now on display in Stockholm.

Appendix D

Useful UK addresses

For advice when you find an underwater site contact:

The Archaeological Diving Unit (ADU)
University of St Andrews
Fife KY 16 9AJ
Tel: 01334 462 919
Fax: 01334 462 921
Email mld@st-andrews.ac.uk

All marine finds recovered in the UK must be reported to:

Receiver of Wreck
The Coastguard Agency
Spring Place
105 Commercial Road
Southampton SO15 1EG
Tel: 01703 329 474
Fax: 01703 329 477

Also report your find to the relevant heritage body. In the UK these are:

Royal Commission on the
Ancient and Historic
Monuments of England (RCHME)
Maritime Section
Kemble Drive
Swindon
Wilts SN2 2GZ
Tel: 01793 414 600
Fax: 01222 826 375

Historic Scotland
Longmore House
Salisbury Place
Edinburgh EH9 1SH
Tel: 0131 668 8764
Fax: 0131 668 8765

Royal Commission on the Ancient
and Historic Monuments of
Scotland (RCAHMS)
John Sinclair House
16 Bernard Terrace
Edinburgh EH18 9NX
Tel: 0131 662 1456
Fax: 0131 662 1477/1499

Environment and Heritage Service
5–33 Hill Street
Belfast BT1 2LA
Tel: 012332 235 000
Fax: 01232 543 111

Welsh Historic Monuments (CADW)
Crown Building
Cathays Park
Cardiff CF1 3NQ
Tel: 01222 500 200
Fax: 01222 826 375

Royal Commission on the Ancient and Historical Monuments of Wales (RCAHMW)
National Monuments Record Centre
Crown Building
Plas Crug
Aberystwyth
Dyfed SY23 2HP
Tel: 01970 614 381
Fax: 01970 627 701

If the site is a military aircraft contact:

The Royal Air Force
Mrs D Sheldon CS (SEC) 2a1
RAF Innsworth
Gloucester, GL3 1EZ
Tel: 01452 712 612 ext 5017/9

For training in the techniques of underwater archaeology contact:

The Nautical Archaeological Society
NAS Training
C/o 19 College Road
HM Naval Base
Portsmouth PO1 3LJ
Tel/Fax: 01706 818 419

NAS Training (Scotland)
Philip Robertson
Lochaline Dive Centre
Lochaline
Morvern
Argyl
PA34 5XT
Tel/Fax: 01967 421 627

For conservation advice and addresses of conservators contact:

The Nautical Archaeological Society
C/o 19 College Road
HM Naval Base
Portsmouth PO1 3LJ
Tel/Fax: 01706 818 419

UK Institute for Conservation (UKIC)
109 The Chandlery
50 Westminster Bridge Road
London SE1 7QY
Tel: 0171 721 8721
Fax: 0171 721 8722

Archaeology Section of UKIC (UKICAS)
109 The Chandlery
50 Westminster Bridge Road
London SE1 7QY
Tel: 0171 721 8721
Fax: 0171 721 8722

English Heritage
23 Savile Row
London W1X 2AB
Tel: 0171 973 30000

Mary Rose Trust
HM College Rd,
Naval Base
Portsmouth PO1 3LX
Tel: 01705 750721

National Maritime Museum
Greenwich
London SE10 9NF
Tel: 0181 858 4422
Fax: 0181 312 6632

National Museum of Wales
Cathays Park
Cardiff CF1 3NP

York Archaeological Trust
Cromwell House
13 Ogleforth
York YO1 2JG
Tel: 01904 612 529
Fax: 01904 637 298

For advice on health and safety (COSHH) matters contact:

HSE Information Centre
Broad Lane
Sheffield S3 7HQ
Tel: 01742 892 345
Fax: 01742 892 333

The Conservation Unit
Museums and Galleries Commission (MGC)
7 St James Square
London SWQ1Y 4JU
Tel: 0171 233 3683

The International Institute for Conservation of Historic and Artistic Works (IIC)
6 Buckingham Street
London WC2 6BA
Tel: 0171 839 5975
Fax: 0171 976 1564

Glossary

Aerated water Conditions where there is a plentiful supply of oxygen that is continually being replenished. (*See* **anoxic**)

Aerobic environments Conditions where biological activity needs a supply of oxygen to take place. (*See* **anaerobic**)

Alloy A mixture of two or more metals.

Anaerobic environments Conditions where biological activity needs an absence of oxygen to take place. Other sources of energy release are used, such as sulphides. (*See* **aerobic**)

Anoxic environments Conditions where there is no oxygen. (*See* **aerated**)

Archaeology The reconstruction of life in the past by the study of material evidence left behind by people, cultures and civilisations. Unlike treasure hunting, in archaeology the emphasis is on the study of people and their way of life, and not on collecting their material possessions for personal gain. (*See* **treasure hunting**)

Backfilling The practice of covering a site after it has been surveyed or excavated.

Biocides Chemicals or substances that stop the growth and activity of micro-organisms, algae and fungi.

Calcification The process by which components of a material, usually bone, are replaced by calcium compounds.

Chilled temperatures In the context of first-aid conservation chilled temperatures are taken to be just above freezing, between 0°C and 4°C. (*See* **refrigeration**)

Concretions Dense masses of hard material that form from corroding iron. They may be found on the surface of any material, or as a layer stretching across a whole site. They are composed mainly of the oxides of iron.

Conservation Interventionist methods aiming to maintain a find in a stable state after it has been recovered. Cleaning and drying are interventionist conservation techniques. (*See* **first aid and restoration**)

Conservator A person who has been trained and qualified in conservation techniques and who understands the ethics and principles involved.

Deionised water Water that has been passed through a deioniser to make it pure. The deioniser attracts and removes ions (components of salts) from the water. It needs to be re-charged at regular intervals. (*See* **distilled water**)

Dendrochronology Dating timbers by examination of their tree rings.

Desalinate Removing salts, usually by flushing them out over a period of time.

Distilled water Water that has been purified by allowing it to boil and the steam collected as it condenses. (*See* **deionised water**)

Electrochemical corrosion Corrosion caused by the flow of electrons. When two touching metals or two areas of a metal are immersed in an electrolyte (a fluid which can conduct electricity, for example sea-water) a current (electrons) flows between them and an electrical cell forms, like a battery. The site where ions are released becomes the anode and corrosion occurs. The other site, the cathode, does not corrode. (*See* **sacrificial anode**)

Electrolytic reduction The conservation process by which harmful salts and corrosion stimulants are removed from a metal by making it the cathode of an electrolytic cell.

First aid The steps of minimum intervention taken to prevent the deterioration of a find following discovery. This usually involves careful packing and storing and involves no change in the state of the find. (*See* **conservation, and restoration**)

Freeze-drying The means by which finds are dried direct from a frozen state. This involves placing the frozen find in a vacuum chamber and gradually allowing the ice formed to change directly into water vapour. By doing this the water phase is eliminated, and with it the risk of surface tension causing damage to degraded fibres and cells. It is used to treat organic finds that would be damaged by normal drying processes.

Graphitisation The process by which cast iron is transformed by corrosion into a matrix of oxidation products and flakes of graphite which were formed during manufacture.

Hard water Water containing high amounts of calcium and magnesium hydrogen carbonates (bicarbonates). It characteristically forms lime scale on kettles. (*See* **soft water**)

Hydrogen reduction An out-dated method of treating marine iron. Iron was heated to high temperatures in a stream of hydrogen in order to stabilise it.

Infra red (IR) IR is invisible radiation emitted by light and heat sources. It can be used to detect the remains of certain inks by photographing a chosen find in the presence of an IR source and recording the image on IR photographic film. The film is then processed like normal photographic film and the image examined.

Inorganic materials Materials and substances that were never part of a living organism. Instead they derive from minerals, metals or synthetic materials. (*See* **organic materials**)

Organic materials Materials and substances that originally came from a living source. (*See* **inorganic materials**)

Organic solvents Liquids with carbon in their molecular structure, for example methylated spirits, alcohol, white spirit (Stoddards solvent) and acetone, used to dissolve other substances such as plastics, adhesives and resins.

pH A measure on a scale of 0 to 14 of the acidity or alkalinity of a liquid. Neutral solutions have a pH of 7. Levels above this are alkaline and below this are acidic. Standard seawater has a pH of 8.2.

Polyethylene glycol (PEG) A wax-like substance that can be dissolved in water and used to consolidate waterlogged wood. It is available in different grades: high grade PEG is hard like bees-wax. Low grades are soft and greasy like Vaseline.

Radiocarbon (C^{14}) The radioactive form of carbon that can be used to date certain finds.

Refrigeration In the context of first-aid conservation keeping finds in a refrigerator at temperatures between 0°C and 4°C.

Relative humidity (RH) The measure of the moisture content of the air, expressed as a percentage of the total amount of moisture the air can hold at that temperature. Cool air can hold less moisture than warm air, so as temperature drops RH increases and the air becomes damper, ultimately resulting in condensation. If the temperature rises RH drops and the air becomes dryer.

Restoration The reconstruction of a find to regain the original shape and condition. This usually involves mending and replacing missing parts. (*See* **first aid and conservation**)

Sacrificial anode A means of protecting a metal, usually iron, from corrosion by placing it in contact with a more reactive metal, such as zinc or aluminium. An electrical cell forms between the two and the anode corrodes in preference to the other, more noble, metal. (*See* **electrochemical corrosion**)

Salinity The amount of salts dissolved in water. Typical water from open seas has a salinity of 35 o/oo (g/kg), although it becomes diluted by freshwater near estuaries. In the Mediterranean seawater is more saline (39 o/oo) and in the Baltic much less (4 o/oo).

Seawater A rich mixture of dissolved salts and microscopic marine organisms (plankton) that has a standard pH of 8.2 and salinity of 35 o/oo, although variations occur throughout the world.

Soft water Water containing low amounts of dissolved magnesium or calcium hydrogen carbonates (bicarbonates). It is usually slightly acidic. (*See* **hard water**)

Treasure hunting In treasure hunting finds are retrieved with little or no regard for their archaeological significance. It is usually, but not always, motivated by the thought of personal gain. (*See* **archaeology**)

X-radiography (x-ray examination) A photographic plate sensitive to X-rays is placed under an object and x-rays are fired at it. Because these rays penetrate materials to different degrees the resultant shadow image on the plate, revealed after processing, can be used to detect the contents of iron concretions. X-rays can be harmful to humans so this is a highly specialised operation. The process is similar to that used by the medical profession to examine fractured limbs.

Bibliography

Allen, A. (ed.) 1995 *Museums and Maritime Archaeology: Dealing with maritime finds.* Cleveland County Archaeology Section and the North of England Museums Service.

Bass, G. F. and Van Doorninck Jr, F. H. 1978 'An eleventh century shipwreck at Serçe Liman, Turkey', *International Journal of Nautical Archaeology* **7**, 119–32.

Clarke, R., Dean, M., Hutchinson, G., McGrail, S. and Squirrell, J. 1993 'Recent work on the R. Hamble wreck near Burlesdon, Hampshire', *International Journal of Nautical Archaeology* **22**, 21–44.

Cronyn, J. M. 1990 *The Elements of Archaeological Conservation*. London: Routledge. (ISBN 0-415-01206-6)

Dean, M., Ferrari, B., Oxley, I., Redknap, M. and Watson, K. (eds) 1995 *Archaeology Underwater. The NAS Guide to Principles and Practice*. London: Archetype and Nautical Archaeology Society. (ISBN 1-873132-25-5)

Guthrie, J. N., Blackall, L. L., Moriarty, D. J. W. and Gesner, P. 1994 'Wrecks and marine microbiology: case study from the *Pandora*', *Bulletin of the Australian Institute for Maritime Archaeology* **18**(2), 19–24.

McCarthy, M. 1988 'SS *Xanthos*: The pre-disturbance assessment, excavation and management of an iron stem shipwreck off the coast of Western Australia', *International Journal of Nautical Archaeology* **17**, 339–47.

Macleod, I. D. 1987 'Conservation of corroded iron artefacts – new methods for on-site preservation and cryogenic deconcreting', *International Journal of Nautical Archaeology* **16**, 49–56.

Macleod, I. D. 1983 'Stabilisation of corroded aluminium', *Studies in Conservation* **28,** 1–7.

Macleod, I. D. 1995 'In situ corrosion studies on the Duart Point wreck, 1994', *International Journal of Nautical Archaeology* **24**, 53–9.

Martin, C. J. M. 1995 'The Cromwellian shipwreck off Duart Point, Mull: an interim report', *International Journal of Nautical Archaeology* **24**, 15–32.

Pearson, C. 1977 'On-site conservation requirements from marine archaeological excavations', *International Journal of Nautical Archaeology*, **6**, 37–46.

Pearson, C. (ed.) 1987 *Conservation of Marine Archaeological Objects*. London: Butterworth-Heinemann. (ISBN 0-408-10668-9)

Robinson, W. 1981 *First Aid for Marine Finds*. London: National Maritime Museum.

Technical reports on conservation may be found in the following journals:
The International Journal of Nautical Archaeology (IJNA) Published by NAS. London. (ISSN 1057-2414)
Studies in Conservation. Published by IIC. London. (ISSN 0039-3630)

Legislation:
The Merchant Shipping Act 1894.
The Protection of Military Remains Act 1986.
The Protection of Wrecks Act 1975.
The Treasure Act 1996 (England and Wales), DCMS, 1997.
The Treasure Act 1996 (Northern Ireland), DCMS, 1997.

Index